T0079743

PUDDING

Edible

Series Editor: Andrew F. Smith

EDIBLE is a revolutionary new series of books dedicated to food and drink that explores the rich history of cuisine. Each book reveals the global history and culture of one type of food or beverage.

Already published

Pudding

A Global History

Jeri Quinzio

REAKTION BOOKS

Published by Reaktion Books Ltd
33 Great Sutton Street
London EC1V 0DX, UK
www.reaktionbooks.co.uk

First published 2012

Printed and bound in China by Eurasia

British Library Cataloguing in Publication Data
Quinzio, Jeri.
Pudding: a global history. – (Edible)
1. Puddings –History. 2. Cooking (Puddings) – History.
3. Puddings – History – Sources
I. Title II. Series
641.8´644-dc23

ISBN 978 1 78023 042 9

Contents

Introduction

Blessed be he that invented pudding.

Henri Misson de Valbourg, *Memoirs*, 1698

Spending Christmas at an English country house did not appeal to Hercule Poirot. The holiday was for children, manor houses were cold and he had better things to do. But in Agatha Christie's story 'The Adventure of the Christmas Pudding', the famed detective was persuaded to take on a case that necessitated spending the holiday at the home of the Lacey family. There he was immersed in the traditions of an old-fashioned English Christmas. 'All the same old things', explained Mrs Lacey to the detective when he arrived, 'the Christmas tree and the stockings hung up and the oyster soup and the turkey . . . and the plum pudding'.

Indeed, the crowning glory of the next day's dinner was the pudding. It was 'a large football of a pudding, a piece of holly stuck in it like a triumphant flag and glorious flames of blue and red rising round it'. However, for Poirot, the pudding had sinister overtones. The night before, he'd found a note in his room warning: 'DON'T EAT NONE OF THE PLUM PUDDING. ONE AS WISHES YOU WELL.' It was not signed. Despite the ominous tone of the note, Poirot accepted a

Pudding in extreme closeup.

helping of the pudding, tasted it and, much to his surprise, found it to be 'delicious'. Of course, eating the pudding led to his solving the mystery.

Christie was not alone in writing pudding into a plot. Authors from Shakespeare to Austen, from Trollope to A. A. Milne have written about pudding in one way or another. It has played a major role in literature, appearing in works as different from one another as *Through the Looking Glass, Casey at the Bat* and *A Christmas Carol*. Authors have used pudding to signify celebration, indulgence and comfort. They've also used it to suggest want, boredom and inequality. An eighteenth-century English writer later identified as Henry Carey used pudding as a symbol of political corruption in a satirical pamphlet. Cartoonists of every era and political persuasion have relished pudding. As an adjective, pudding's meanings are diametrically different. A dull, thickset lump of a person is described as a pudding-head or pudding boy. Yet arriving 'in pudding time' means coming just in time for dinner. What could be better?

Christmas pudding often symbolizes unchanging tradition and hospitality, as it did in *The Adventure of the Christmas Pudding*. Rice pudding, on the other hand, is as likely to signify monotony as solace. In A. A. Milne's poem 'Rice Pudding' it's dull

Hablot Knight Browne ('Phiz') (1885–1892), 'A Merry Christmas': this book illustration depicts Father Christmas and everything held essential to the season.

9

and repetitive, the same old nursery dessert served to the child who knew that downstairs in the dining room something much better was to be had. A far cry from M.F.K. Fisher's image of rice pudding: she said it was 'pleasant to eat in bed with Music-till-Dawn turned on low-low. It will bring sweet dreams.'[1]

It's no wonder pudding has such a variable image. It's a versatile dish. Depending on the time, place and person speaking, a pudding may be a meaty mixture stuffed into a casing made from an animal's intestine, rather like a sausage. Or it may be a stodgy combination of flour and water boiled like a dumpling and served to fill up rather than delight. At the other end of the spectrum, puddings resemble fruitcake, resplendent with raisins, figs, dates, nuts and spices. Puddings can be last-minute desserts or they may be made weeks (or even months) ahead of time and aged until a special occasion calls for them. They may be doused with brandy and set ablaze for serving. They may be an extravaganza of exotic ingredients

John Philips, 'Emancipation Pudding; or, Who are the Carvers', *c.* 1829, etching. Some for church; some for state.

In 'Cutting their pudding before it's baked,' one of Jay N. 'Ding' Darling's pointed pen and ink editorial cartoons from 1940, Germany takes the largest share of the pudding.

or a good way to use up lacklustre leftovers. They may be boiled, steamed, baked, slow-cooked in a Crockpot, zapped in a microwave or not cooked at all. Also known as pudding is an array of lush, silken creams and custards, rich with eggs and milk or cream. They range from crème brûlée to baked custard. In one of their many variations, they can also be made

In 'Pudding Time', George Cruikshank's etching of 1827, the late arrival shows perfect timing.

as sauces for a steamed pudding. A pudding for a pudding, in other words.

Pudding is so many different dishes to so many people that most dictionaries fail to give it its due. It is a simple word. With just seven letters, it's easy to pronounce and spell. Yet it defies strict definition. *The Random House Dictionary* calls pudding, rather unappealingly, a 'thick, soft dessert, typically containing flour or some other thickener'. That omits the many meat, fish and other savoury puddings that are served as a first course, main course or side dish rather than a dessert. It also neglects the fact that puddings now thought of as desserts were often first courses in earlier times. The generic dictionary on my computer defines pudding as 'a sweet cooked dessert with a smooth creamy texture, typically consisting of flour, milk, eggs and flavoring'. That not only ignores savoury puddings, but also the decidedly unsmooth fruit-filled and bread-based puddings. The online dictionary does give pudding a second meaning: in the UK, it's 'the dessert course of a meal'. In Britain and some other English-speaking countries, though not the United States, pudding became a generic word for dessert early in the twentieth century. The answer to the question 'What's for pudding?' or, colloquially, 'What's for pud, mum?' may be anything from apple pie to an actual pudding.

According to the *Oxford English Dictionary* the word 'pudding' dates to the thirteenth century when it referred to the stomach or entrails of a pig, sheep or other animal, stuffed with a mixture of minced meat, suet, oatmeal and seasonings. A kind of sausage, it was usually boiled. By the sixteenth century, the word was also being used for the contents of people's bellies, often in a violent context. If someone plunged his sword into your belly, your puddings would spill out. Less violently, the OED defines pudding as:

> A boiled, steamed, or baked dish made with various sweet
> or (sometimes) savoury ingredients added to the mixture
> typically including milk, eggs, and flour (or other starchy

Puddings have long been ubiquitous images on postcards and Christmas cards. This is an early 20th-century postcard by the American artist Ellen H. Clapsaddle.

ingredients such as suet, rice, semolina, etc.), or enclosed within a crust made from such a mixture.

In this book, I consider pudding from its sausage-like beginnings to the sumptuous dessert puddings that developed over time. I recount the stories behind many iconic puddings – from blood to bread, from rice to plum. Since creams and custards have different traditions, they won't be part of the story; wonderful as they are, they deserve a book all their own. Most countries have puddings that are important to their traditions and culture, and these will be discussed throughout the book. However, it is in Great Britain where pudding shines. I agree with Monsieur Henri Misson de Valbourg, a Frenchman who wrote about his travels in England in the seventeenth century. De Valbourg found puddings difficult to describe, since the English 'make them fifty several ways'. Pudding is, he wrote, a manna 'that hits the palates of all sorts of people; a manna, better than that of the wilderness, because the people are never weary of it'; 'Ah, what an excellent thing is an English pudding!'[2]

I
A Pudding Chronology

Plots and politics may hurt us, but Pudding cannot.

Attributed to Henry Carey, *A Learned Dissertation on Dumpling*, 1726

A Learned Dissertation on Dumpling was published as a satirical pamphlet aimed at the political intrigues of eighteenth-century England. But the author was so convincing in his knowledge of puddings that it is read today by those who are more concerned with cooking than with corruption. Published anonymously in 1726 and now attributed to the author and playwright Henry Carey, the work criticized historians 'who eat so much pudding, yet have been so Ungrateful to the first Professors of this most noble Science, as not to find 'em a Place in History'.[1]

Despite Carey's scorn, we know that pudding's place in history dates back to ancient times. One of the earliest mentions of pudding comes from Homer's *Odyssey* and describes a blood pudding roasted in a pig's stomach. Animal stomachs and intestines, thoroughly cleaned, were among the first cooking vessels. Cooks prepared an assortment of mixtures in them. The main ingredient might be blood or it might be meat, rice, bread or marrow. It would be mixed with a fat, usually suet, the hard white fat found on the kidneys of cattle.

In addition, anything from almonds to cream, dates or eggs would be added along with an assortment of herbs and spices depending on the imagination and the resources of the cook. After stuffing the mixture into the intestines, the cooks boiled the puddings in a pot suspended over the fire. Occasionally, rather than being boiled, the filled intestine was roasted within the animal, but this was usually done for a dramatic presentation at a feast rather than for a family's dinner.

Black, or blood, puddings and other meat puddings developed as a way to preserve the perishable blood, meat and offal of slaughtered animals. When seasoned, packed into a stomach or intestine, and cooked, they kept longer. The fact that the puddings were tasty and filling, in addition to being practical, is probably the reason they are still made and enjoyed. White puddings were made and cooked like black puddings but did not include blood; they were usually made with a light meat such as veal, chicken or pork, along with a

Jacques Phillippe Le Bas, *La Boudinière* (the black pudding maker), *c.* 1747, etching. In 18th-century France, the whole family was involved in making blood pudding.

filler of oats, rice or bread. Those who were well-off sweetened their puddings and added butter, currants, raisins, eggs or spices to them. Over time, as more dried fruits, sugar and spices were added to these mixtures, these puddings developed into the steamed sweet puddings, like the renowned plum pudding, that we prize today.

The Pudding Cloth

Puddings made in stomachs or intestines have some obvious disadvantages. Guts are difficult to clean thoroughly and challenging to fill. Sir Kenelm Digby, writing in the mid-seventeenth century, advised that the guts be well washed and scoured and then soaked for three days and three nights, 'shifting the water twice every day: and every time you shift the water, scour them first with Water and Salt'.[2] Guts are also only obtainable at slaughtering time when the parts are fresh and intact, and their use is limited by the number of animals slaughtered.

Cooks were freed of these limitations during the seventeenth century when, according to printed records, pudding cloths were developed. (No doubt the cloths were being used for some time before anyone thought to write about them.) The cloths made pudding preparation easier and more practical. A pudding cloth was simply a sturdy piece of fabric, closely woven so that water wouldn't seep in. The pudding mixture was poured or placed in the centre of the cloth. Then the four corners were tied up in a secure knot, allowing some extra room if the pudding was expected to swell, tying it tightly if it was not. The resulting bag of pudding could be suspended from a stick across a large stewpot and submerged in water or broth, then boiled for a few hours. Or it could be

The pudding bag transformed pudding-making.

placed atop a saucer or rack in the pot – so that the bottom of the bag would not touch the pot and thereby burn – and submerged in the boiling water. When the pudding was ready, the bag was removed and dipped into cold water to release the pudding, and then turned out onto a platter.

Vegetables and meat were usually boiled in the pot with the pudding. If the family had a roast, the pudding might be boiled and then sliced and placed in a dripping pan under the roast. The well-to-do served the pudding along with other dishes as part of the main course. The less well-off ate the pudding first to satisfy hunger before the more expensive meat and other foods were served. Course distinctions had no meaning for the very poor; for them, a boiled pudding was often the only course.

Cookbook writers stressed the need to use spotlessly clean pudding bags and often included instructions on soaking and washing them. Isabella Beeton, who was one of the mid-nineteenth century's most influential cookery writers, offered the following instructions in the 1861 edition of her *Book of Household Management*:

Boiled Puddings.

GENERAL DIRECTIONS.

A boiled pudding, from Eliza Acton's *Modern Cookery for Private Families, Reduced to a System of Easy Practice, in a Series of Carefully Tested Receipts* (1885).

Scrupulous attention should be paid to the cleanliness of pudding-cloths, as, from neglect in this particular, the outsides of boiled puddings frequently taste very disagreeably. As soon as possible after it is taken off the pudding, it should be soaked in water, and then well washed, without soap, unless it be very greasy. It should be dried out of doors, then folded up and kept in a dry place. When wanted for use, dip it in boiling water, and dredge it slightly with flour.

The importance that was attached to the care and cleaning of pudding cloths helps to explain why Charles Dickens compared the scent of pudding to a laundry in this passage from *A Christmas Carol* (1843):

" *Will that pudding be long?* "
" *No, sir, it will be round; or, to be more precise, spherical.* "

A small helping of early 20th-century pudding humour. Publishers Bamforth & Co. Ltd were known for their witty postcards. The artist is not credited.

Hallo! A great deal of steam! The pudding was out of the copper. A smell like a washing-day! That was the cloth. A smell like an eating-house and a pastrycook's next door to each other, with a laundress's next door to that! That was the pudding!

Pudding Pans and Pudding Moulds

During the seventeenth century, puddings also came to be cooked in basins, which were deep bowls with thick rims. The basins were greased and filled with the pudding mixture, and a cloth was tied either over the top of the basin or over the entire bowl. They were then placed in a pot of simmering water up to the rim of the basin, not submerged, and the pot was covered so that the pudding would steam rather than boil.

Those who were fortunate enough to have an oven built into the side of their fireplace or to have a separate bread

Modern-day pudding moulds.

oven could bake puddings. They often lined the pan with puff pastry before filling it or garnished the rim of the basin with pastry. Alternatively they might just pour the mixture into a greased basin and bake it. More like pies than puddings, they were often referred to as pudding-pies, blurring the line between the two. They may be the origin of the popular phrase 'as easy as pudding pie'.

In the nineteenth century, tin pudding moulds became available. Since these were easier to use than cloths, even women without kitchen help could make steamed puddings, and they did. The new utensils allowed them to expand their repertoires dramatically. Now that they could make puddings any time, they made them all the time, 'from the simple suet dumpling up to the most complicated Christmas production', as Mrs Beeton wrote.

A Plethora of Puddings

Cooks around the world made puddings, but English cooks made them their speciality. Their love of puddings may have been influenced by the fact that the German-speaking George I (1660–1727) enjoyed them so much that he became known as the Pudding King. Although he was not well-liked, his love of puddings, especially sweet puddings, helped popularize the dish. As Carey wrote in *A Learned Dissertation on Dumpling*, 'Let not Englishmen therefore be asham'd of the Name of Pudding-Eaters; but, on the contrary, let it be their Glory.' And so it was. Pudding recipes proliferated in English cookbooks. In the revised edition of her book *The Art of Cookery Made Plain and Easy* (1796), Hannah Glasse had more than 70 pudding recipes. By 1861, Mrs Beeton had more than 90. By then, in England, a meal was hardly a meal without a pudding.

J. Josephs, 'A Cut', *c.* 1818, hand-coloured etching. The largest slice goes to the first to carve.

Cooks made sweet puddings as well as savoury ones, dainty puddings and hefty ones. Some continued to use guts as containers, but more often they boiled, steamed or baked their puddings in bags, basins, moulds, pie pans, or even in small, buttered teacups. Those who didn't have lovely fluted moulds or pudding dishes made do. In an American manuscript cookbook begun in 1900, the writer said she cooked her plum pudding in 'a tin pail placed in a kettle of boiling water'. Another writer suggested 'little granite or enamel buckets'. Years later, coffee cans became perfect steaming vessels.

In the first half of the twentieth century, both published cookbooks and manuscript books were filled with recipes for pudding and accompanying sauces. Home cooks made a variety of puddings; street vendors sold simple ones; and chefs

Some of Mrs Beeton's many delectable puddings, from the 1895 edition of her *Book of Household Management*.

made complex, beautifully presented ones. Puddings were served in pubs and school dining halls and featured on the menus of fine dining restaurants like Simpson's-in-the-Strand in London and Locke-Ober in Boston. Cooks made puddings from simple flour-and-milk batters combined with fruits, like the French clafoutis. They made rice puddings that ranged from plain mixtures of rice and milk to *riz à l'impératrice*, rich with whipped cream and preserved fruit. Bread puddings could be thrifty combinations of stale bread and milk as well as extravagant concoctions of rich cake and custard. Cooks topped puddings with meringue, or served them with custard sauces, sauces made with wine, with beaten butter and sugar, or with fruit syrups. At the very least they sprinkled sugar or poured butter over the puddings. Plum puddings were as much a part of Christmas as the stockings hung by the fire. 'Indian' puddings were essential to New England's Thanksgiving dinners. Pudding's place in history seemed secure.

2

Puddings in Black and White

Still puddings run deep.

May Byron, *Puddings, Pastries and Sweet Dishes*, 1929

What could be a better symbol of the darker side of the human character than blood pudding? Today, we avoid the sight of blood, and many people are revolted by the idea of consuming it. Some religions forbid it. We hardly see a drop on our meats, and the butcher wearing a bloodied apron has disappeared from view. Even in the past, when blood pudding was much more common than it is now, writers served it up in their more macabre stories.

The aptly named Brothers Grimm featured a human blood pudding in their story 'The Juniper Tree'. In this grisly tale, a wicked stepmother kills her stepson and turns him into a blood pudding, which she serves to his father. Although in the end the stepmother is killed and the son miraculously returned to life, most readers will shudder at the thought of eating blood pudding afterwards.

Earlier, a less grisly but equally bizarre story was told in 'Trimalchio's Feast', the Roman tale that has come to symbolize the excesses of the Empire. Sometimes taken literally, the story appears in *The Satyricon* (first century AD) and was intended to satirize and ridicule the flamboyance of *nouveau riche* dining. The author, today believed to be Petronius, a courtier to the emperor Nero, describes a dinner party at which an arriviste named Trimalchio tries to dazzle his guests with such exotic foods as dormice seasoned with poppy seeds and honey, peafowl eggs made of pastry and filled with spiced garden warblers, and a wild boar filled with live thrushes that fly about the room when the boar is carved.

The dinner's most dramatic moment occurs when three large live pigs are brought into the dining room and the guests are asked to choose one for their meal. Shortly after, and much too soon to have prepared such an animal properly, an enormous roasted pig is brought in on a platter. Trimalchio flies into a rage: the pig had not been gutted before being cooked, he claims, berating the servant. To the horror of his guests, Trimalchio insists that the pig be gutted then and there on the table. When the servant slits open the pig,

Black puddings are as popular as ever in the Lancashire region.

plump, fully roasted black puddings tumble out, leaving the guests amazed and relieved.

Although puddings were sometimes roasted inside animals, most people could not afford such an extravagance. They just boiled their puddings in a pot. In the seventeenth and eighteenth centuries, black or blood puddings were made with the blood of pigs, geese, lambs, sheep and calves. Pig's blood was generally favoured as pigs were more plentiful and less costly to raise. British puddings were usually made with oatmeal or grated bread as filler. Other ingredients varied; suet, cream, spinach, parsley, endive, sweet marjoram, strawberry leaves, fennel seed, salt, pepper and cloves were all added to puddings. The seventeenth-century writer Robert May had a recipe for 'puddings of blood after the Italian fashion', using hog's blood.[1] The addition of grated cheese set it apart and, apparently, made it Italian, although he didn't specify the type of cheese. However, cooks often kept their own particular recipe a well-guarded secret.

Regions and towns, as well as individual cooks, boasted of special puddings at this time. The Outer Hebrides in Scotland and in particular the town of Stornoway were famous for a black pudding known as *marag dubh* in Scottish Gaelic. The city of Cork, in Ireland, was known for its drisheen (*drisín*), a blood pudding made with a combination of sheep and beef blood. Drisheen was simmered in milk and served with a white sauce made with plenty of butter. Lancashire, and in particular the town of Bury, was famed for its unique black pudding. It is still a local speciality.

Black puddings were sold by street vendors, served in fine dining restaurants and made at home. Still popular today, they are also an essential part of the famed full English breakfast, which also includes eggs, bacon, grilled tomatoes and fried bread.

In Other Worlds

Other countries have their own blood puddings. In France, *boudin noir* is traditionally made with pig's blood and fried or grilled after its initial boil; but each region, if not each butcher, has its own version. A speciality of Alsace is *zungenwurst*, made with pieces of pig's tongue wrapped in bacon and cooked in an ox intestine. In Brittany, prunes are added to the *boudin noir*; in Flanders, raisins; in the Auvergne, chestnuts. Normandy, famed for the quality of its apples, serves them as an accompaniment to black pudding. Mashed potatoes are its usual accompaniment in other parts of the country.

Boudin Antillais, a speciality of the islands of Martinique and Guadeloupe in the French West Indies, is a blood pudding that is cooked in a broth flavoured with onions, peppers, chives and other herbs and spices. It is traditionally served as a Christmas dish. The French influence is also apparent in Louisiana. Although blood pudding has never been as popular in the United States as it is in Europe, Louisiana's *boudin* is an exception. Called *boudin rouge* rather than *noir*, it is made with pork fat and blood, onions, garlic, and salt, pepper, allspice, cayenne, nutmeg, cloves and *fines herbes*.

The filler as well as the flavourings differentiate puddings. In Spain, blood pudding is usually mixed with rice, and its other ingredients include pine nuts, cloves, anise and cinnamon. The pudding is called *morcilla*, or *morcilla de Burgo* after a town in northern Spain that is known for its excellent blood pudding. *Morcilla* is served as a main course or as tapas, and smoked *morcilla* is essential to the pork and bean stew from Asturias called *fabada Asturiana*.

Blutwurst is Germany's blood pudding, and barley is its filler. When it is served with apple sauce and mashed potatoes, it is called *Himmel und Erde*, or heaven and earth. In Italy, different regions have their own recipes and names for blood pudding. However, *budino nero* is not a blood pudding as its literal translation would suggest, but rather a chocolate bread pudding. The most universal name for Italian blood pudding is *sanguinaccio* and in addition to a savoury dish, it may also be a sweet one. One sweet version, from Puglia, is made with pig's blood, milk, sugar, chocolate, cocoa, cloves, cinnamon, lemon or orange peel and butter. The mixture is simmered slowly in a bain-marie, rather than boiled in intestines, then served in decorative cups and topped with pine nuts. My grandmother made a blood jam with similar ingredients and served it atop the Italian wafer-like cookies called *pizzelle*. We children loved it until we were told that it was made with pig's blood.

White Puddings

In addition to puddings made with blood or red meats, a range of savoury and also sweet white puddings were made using light meats such as chicken, pork or veal, while some were made with fish. Such puddings date back to medieval times in Europe and Asia.

Blancmange was originally a pudding made with shredded chicken or fish, thickened with grated stag's horn or rice, and flavoured with almonds. Today, in most countries, it has evolved into a simple almond cream pudding, but a version closer to the original survives today, indeed thrives, in Turkey. There the pudding called *tavuk göʻsü*, which means chicken breast, is made with finely shredded chicken breast, rice, milk and sugar, flavoured with cinnamon. Served as a dessert, it's very much like its ancient precursor.

One of the best-known white puddings is France's *boudin blanc*. It originated during the Middle Ages when churchgoers would warm up with a milky gruel after attending Midnight Mass on Christmas Eve. Pork butchers came up with the idea of adding eggs and ground meat to the gruel and stuffing the mixture into intestines to cook. Gradually, the new dish became the time-honoured one. Typically made with finely shredded white meats such as pork, chicken, veal or fish, along with cream, eggs, flour or breadcrumbs and spices, it was stuffed into intestines and poached, fried or baked. One variation, *boudin à la Richelieu*, was cooked in moulds rather than intestines and served with a sauce enhanced with truffles. *Boudin blanc aux pruneaux* was surrounded with prunes and baked. In France, it is still traditional to enjoy *boudin blanc* at Christmastime.

British white puddings date back to at least the fifteenth century and were often made from pig's livers mixed with cream, eggs, breadcrumbs, raisins and dates. Flavourings included cloves, mace, saffron and sugar. The British also made white puddings without meat, other than suet. *The Good Hous-wives Treasurie*, published in 1588, had a recipe for white pudding made with grated bread, currants, egg yolks, nutmeg, cinnamon, sugar, salt and beef suet. Elizabeth Raffald's cookbook *The Experienced English Housekeeper* (1769) contained just one white pudding recipe, which she called 'White Puddings in Skins'. Meatless, it was made with cooked rice combined with almonds beaten with rose water, currants, lard, eggs, sugar, nutmeg, cinnamon and mace. In Scotland, white pudding made with oatmeal is called mealie pudding.

An American white pudding recipe from one of the country's most popular cookbooks, *Buckeye Cookery and Practical Housekeeping* by Estelle Woods Wilcox, was called 'Grandma Thompson's White Pudding'. It consisted of nothing more than flour and suet seasoned with salt and pepper, and stuffed into 'beef-skins (entrails cleansed like pork-skins for sausage), half a yard or less in length'. These were boiled and then hung up to dry. When wanted, a portion was cut off, boiled again, and then placed before the fire to crisp. The recipe appeared in the 1877 edition of the book, but Wilcox wrote that the pudding was served at 'quilting frolics' and 'logrollings' one hundred years before.

Pudding revels

In France and Britain today, blood puddings are the stuff of festivals. Britain's takes place in Manchester and is called the World Black Pudding Throwing Championships. Blood sausages are stuffed into ladies' tights and hurled at a 20-foot-high (6-m) stack of Yorkshire puddings; the contestant who knocks the most puddings off the stack wins. The event is said to be based on a battle between the armies of the Houses of Lancaster and York during the Wars of the Roses. It seems the soldiers ran out of ammunition and began hurling food at each other. Now they hurl puddings at puddings instead.

In France, a *Foire au boudin* is held in Normandy in March each year. There, rather than toss puddings, they eat them. An international contest to find the best black pudding, the event is hosted by the *Confrérie des Chevaliers du Goûte Boudin* (Brotherhood of the Knights of the Blood Sausage) and attracts hundreds of contestants each year.

3
Meat Pudding

Great chieftain o' the pudding-race!
Robert Burns, 'Address to a Haggis', 1786

Of all the meat puddings in the world, none is more famous than the Scottish haggis. The *Oxford English Dictionary* defines haggis as:

> A dish consisting of the heart, lungs, and liver of a sheep, calf, etc. (or sometimes of the tripe and chitterlings), minced with suet and oatmeal, seasoned with salt, pepper, onions, etc., and boiled like a large sausage in the maw of the animal.

But this brief definition hardly does justice to the 'great chieftain o' the pudding-race'. More than a mere dish, haggis is a national institution in Scotland, albeit a controversial one. Despite its association with Scotland, the first haggis recipes appeared in English, not Scottish, cookbooks. Treated with reverence and ceremony by its aficionados, it is subjected to ridicule by those who don't appreciate it. For every person who loves haggis, there's another who finds its ingredients and its aroma repulsive.

One of the earliest haggis recipes was published in England in *The Good Hous-wives Treasurie* in 1588. Called 'A Haggas Pudding', the recipe was listed, without comment, after 'How to make a Lenton Pudding' and before 'How to make Sausages'. The recipe began: 'Take the haggas of a Calfe, perboyle him, and when he is cold choppe him very small'. 'He' was then mixed with grated bread, egg yolks, herbs, currants, nutmeg and salt. There was no information as to how the pudding should be cooked or served. At the time, haggis was simply one of many puddings, not one that warranted any pomp or ceremony. It was a commonplace and, more important, it could be an economical dish.

A century later, Robert May included three haggis recipes in *The Accomplisht Cook* under the heading 'Sheeps Haggas Puddings'. The first was made with oatmeal, suet, spices, eggs and butter. Since it contained no meat, apart from beef or mutton suet, he said it could be made without the suet for a fasting day. The second was also primarily oatmeal; suet, cream, spices, onion and herbs were added and it was cooked in the sheep's stomach. The final recipe called for calf's paunch (stomach), chaldrons (entrails) or muggets (intestines), cleaned, boiled and chopped. These were mixed with ingredients that included grated bread, eggs, various herbs and spices, currants and dates. The pudding was boiled, either in a napkin or a calf's paunch, and served with sugar, beaten butter and sliced almonds.

Hannah Glasse called the pudding 'Scotch Haggas'. She had two recipes. The first called for the 'lights, heart, and chitterlings of a calf' along with suet, flour or oatmeal, salt and pepper. She said some cooks added cream, mace, cloves or nutmeg, and remarked 'all-spice is very good in it'. Her second recipe, titled 'To make it sweet with Fruit', added currants, raisins and half a pint of sack (wine) to the first recipe.

Both were boiled in a calf's bag. The second recipe concluded: 'You must carry it to table in the bag it was boiled in.'[1]

All Hail the Haggis

The Scottish poet Robert Burns used the plainspoken dialect of the Scottish peasant to create poetry, and in 1786 he made this plain pudding the subject of what would become one of his most famous poems, 'Address to a Haggis'. Following are two of the eight stanzas:

> Fair fa' your honest, sonsie face,
> Great chieftain o' the pudding-race!
> Aboon them a' yet tak your place,
> Painch, tripe, or thairm:
> Weel are ye wordy o' a grace
> As lang's my arm.
> . . .
> His knife see rustic Labour dight,
> An' cut you up wi' ready sleight,
> Trenching your gushing entrails bright,
> Like ony ditch;
> And then, O what a glorious sight,
> Warm-reekin', rich!

The standard English version is:

> All hail your honest rounded face,
> Great chieftain of the pudding race!
> Above them all you take your place,
> Beef, tripe, or lamb:
> You're worthy of a grace

A whole haggis with neeps, tatties and whisky is the classic menu for Robert Burns's birthday.

As long as my arm.

. . .

His knife the rustic goodman wipes,
To cut you through with all his might,
Revealing your gushing entrails bright,
Like any ditch;
And then, what a glorious sight,
Warm, welcome, rich.

Sanctified by Burns, haggis, accompanied by much ceremony, became the traditional food of Hogmanay, as the
Scottish New Year celebration is known. According to the ritual, a kilted bagpiper heralds the pudding's arrival at the table,
and the drink of the evening is, of course, Scotch whisky.
The birthday of Robert Burns, 25 January, has become an
occasion for more haggis and ceremonies throughout the
world. Today, after the haggis is borne aloft into the dining
room to the accompaniment of a bagpiper, a designated
orator recites the famous poem. At the beginning of the third
stanza, when the person entrusted with the duty says, 'His knife
see rustic Labour dight / An' cut you up wi' ready sleight', he
plunges a knife into the pudding and spills its contents out to
the delight of the guests.

Neeps and tatties (turnips and potatoes) are usually
served alongside the pudding, and other traditional Scottish
foods make up the rest of the menu. Guests often dress in
Scottish regalia. Toasting the pudding with a dram of whisky
is de rigueur, and toasting Robert Burns, the host and, if the
party is not exclusively male as was once traditional, the
hostess as well as many of the guests is a good excuse for
enjoying more of the Scotch. Haggis, sliced and sautéed but
served sans pipers, is also eaten at ordinary meals including
breakfast. It is produced commercially today, and a vegetarian

A conceited little
Boaster..to pretend
to be weigh'd against
me.: does he think
I eat Beef and
pudding for
nothing.

Pub Decr 1803 by W. Holland Nº 11 Cockspur Street London.

BRITANNIA *weighing the* FATE *of* EUROPE;
or
JOHN BULL *too heavy for* BUONAPARTE.

'Britannia weighing the Fate of Europe, or John Bull too heavy for
Buonaparte', 1803, hand-coloured etching. Thanks to beef and pudding,
John Bull easily outweighs Napoleon.

version is made with lentils, black beans, oatmeal, onions and other vegetables.

The Meat of the Matter

In the seventeenth century, the ingredients that made up haggis were not unusual for a pudding. All sorts of meats – from mutton to cow's feet, from hog's liver to turkey – were turned into puddings. May made a pudding from a heifer's udder. He boiled the udder, minced it and then mixed it with almond paste, breadcrumbs, eggs, cream, minced beef suet, herbs, bone marrow, currants, sugar, saffron, nutmeg, cinnamon and diced preserved pears. He wrapped the mixture in a pudding cloth, tied it up like a ball and boiled it until done. When he turned it out onto the serving dish, he poured beaten butter over it and stuck almonds, dates or candied lemon, orange or citron peel into it. Finally, he poured orange juice over it all.

The combination of meat and sweet was typical. Many puddings of the late seventeenth and early eighteenth centuries were both savoury and sweet, and the mixtures reveal the start of puddings' gradual shift towards the sweet end of the spectrum. For example, hack or hackin pudding was a traditional sweet Christmas dish of the northwest of England and, in at least one recipe, the meat was an afterthought. That recipe appeared in *The Country Housewife and Lady's Director*, written by Richard Bradley, a professor of botany at Cambridge University, and published in 1728. Bradley attributed the recipe to a 'Gentleman in Cumberland'. The pudding's ingredients included beef suet, apples, sugar, salt, spice, lemon peel, currants, salt and oatmeal that had been steeped in milk overnight. Bradley suggested adding some beaten eggs as

Contented in his present State.   Surrounded by his Family.   Now view the horrid sad Reverse:
Behold JOHN BULL supremely great.   Joining their Song with merry Glee. The Leveller's — Republic's Curse,
With each domestic Blessing.   They make his Mans'on ring;   Frenchmen's new fangled Laws.
No anxious Cares do him molest.   But if he's rous'd when Cause is good. And if there's dealt of abuse then pray,
His Minds at Ease his Heart's at Rest. To the last drop he'll spill his Blood. Look at the starv'd and lifeless day.
With Comforts past expecting.   For ENGLAND and his KING.   Tears Dagger Rope and Straw.

'John Bull in his Glory'. This 18th-century hand-coloured engraving shows a happy, well-fed family enjoying a plum pudding and roast beef, quintessential English dishes.

well. The ingredients were mixed together and then put in the 'Bag or Paunch of a Calf' and boiled 'till they are enough'. At the end of the recipe Bradley wrote: 'I had forgot to say, that with the rest of the Ingredients, there should be some Lean of tender Beef minced small.'

In 'Admiration', a hand-coloured etching by Thomas Rowlandson of 1800, a hungry boy yearns for a pudding.

many, roast beef was a rare indulgence. In fact, particularly during the nineteenth century, any fresh meat was a luxury. Ordinary families were more likely to be looking for ways to make a few small pieces feed everyone than they were to be serving large joints of meat.

In her lovely trilogy, *Lark Rise to Candleford* (1941–5), about life among the rural poor in Oxfordshire at the end of the nineteenth century, Flora Thompson said that sometimes on a Sunday or a special occasion, 'six-pennyworth of pieces would be bought to make a meat pudding' called a 'toad': 'The meat was enclosed whole in a suet crust and well boiled. That preserved the delicious juices of the meat and provided a good pudding into the bargain.'

Lacking any meat, the pudding might be sweet. But that did not make it a dessert. Thompson wrote:

> On ordinary days the pudding would be a roly-poly containing fruit, currants, or jam; but it still appeared as a first course, the idea being that it took the edge off the appetite.

Lacking even fruit or jam, the pudding might consist of nothing more than suet dough. It would be boiled in the cauldron along with the vegetables, which saved on fuel, and a plain pudding could take the place of bread on the table. After it was boiled, the pudding might be sliced and put on the grill to brown. If meat were roasting on the spit, its juices added flavour to the pudding slices.

Those who didn't have enough money for beef might be able to afford pork. A pig was often the only animal a family could keep since it had the advantage of foraging for itself or eating table scraps. As a result, a pig was highly valued. Thompson explained:

> During its lifetime, the pig was an important member of the family, and its health and condition were regularly reported in letters to children away from home, together with news of their brothers and sisters.

When slaughtered, the pig provided blood, lard, pork and bacon. The bacon appeared on the table with great regularity, albeit in small amounts. The hot meal of the day, served in early evening when the men came in from the fields and the children were home from school, was a simple one for Thompson's family and neighbours.

> Everything was cooked in the one utensil; the square of bacon, amounting to little more than a taste each; cabbage, or other green vegetables in one net, potatoes in another, and the roly-poly swathed in a cloth. It sounds a haphazard method in these days of gas and electric cookers; but it answered its purpose, for, by carefully timing the putting in of each item and keeping the simmering of the pot well regulated, each item was kept intact and an appetising meal was produced. The water in which the food had been cooked, the potato parings, and other vegetable trimmings were the pig's share.

Boiling up an economical meal in one pot was not unusual, nor did the practice end completely with the advent of ovens. An advertisement for a three-tier aluminium steamer ran in *Woman's Life* magazine on 20 February 1926. The steamer was used in much the same way as Thompson's pot. The advertisement copy read:

> Now that winter is really here, we can indulge ourselves with savoury meat puddings – our steamer makes the suet crust deliciously mellow and appetising – and its upper storeys cook potatoes in their jackets and a generous allowance of brussels sprouts to perfection, with a minimum of trouble on our part.[1]

Sweet Suet

Suet puddings were sold in shops and, like everything from eels to hot cross buns, hawked on the streets of London during the nineteenth century. One of the most common street puddings was plum duff, a boiled suet pudding made with raisins and sold for a halfpenny. (The word 'duff' was a Northern English pronunciation of 'dough'.) The young costermongers, or street sellers, were fond of the pudding, and when they heard that someone was selling plum duff with more raisins than usual, they made sure their route took them in the seller's direction so they could buy a slice.

Suet puddings made with raisins or currants were ubiquitous. The puddings might be boiled in cloths, steamed in moulds or baked. Slight variations in the recipe produced different names as well as different puddings. Spotted dick was a particular favourite of schoolchildren. Made with suet dough spread with raisins and sugar, it is rolled into a log like a jelly roll and steamed. Spotted dog is essentially the same but the raisins, or spots, are mixed into the dough. Boiled baby, another raisin and suet pudding, was well loved despite its off-putting name. Described in Patrick O'Brian's historical novel *The Nutmeg of Consolation* as 'a superb suet pudding', it was Captain Jack Aubrey's 'favourite form of food'.

All sorts of ingredients can be mixed into suet dough. Admiral's pudding is made with mixed dried fruit and golden syrup, while Granny's Irish pudding contains marmalade, ginger, rum and Guinness. When suet dough is spread with jam or marmalade, rolled up and steamed, it is called jam roly-poly. Mincemeat, lemon curd, golden syrup or apples sometimes takes the place of the jam.

Cooks also line pudding moulds with suet dough and fill the centres with a near-infinite variety of mixtures. The filling

Paul Sandby, 'A Pudding a Pudding a Hot Pudding', 1760, etching. Hot puddings were cried on the streets of 18th-century London along with everything from apples to oranges.

for rhubarb hat pudding is fresh rhubarb, breadcrumbs and ginger, while blackberry exeter was filled with a mix of blackberries and chopped apples. Sussex, also known as Suffolk, pond pudding contains a whole lemon covered with butter and sugar; the pudding is steamed and turned out onto a deep

Sussex pond pudding spills over with the tart sweetness of lemons.

dish. When sliced, a lush buttery lemon sauce – the pond – flows out.

In 1908 Beatrix Potter, the author known for her delightful Peter Rabbit books, wrote a less appealing story called *The Roly-poly Pudding*. In the story, an old rat captures little Tom Kitten and decides he would make a good pudding. The rat, Samuel Whiskers, asks his wife, Anna Maria, to make a 'kitten dumpling roly-poly pudding for my dinner'. Although Tom Kitten is covered in soot from climbing up the chimney, Anna

Maria rolls him up in dough and prepares to boil the pudding. Fortunately, Tom is rescued and returns home before meeting that fate. But his mother salvages the dough and makes a pudding with 'currants in it to hide the smuts', or sooty marks. This is one of literature's less appetizing puddings.

Scotland's Own Suet Pud

Clootie pudding, also known as a clootie dumpling, is a speciality of Scotland and is named for the cloot, or cloth, it was steamed in. Still made today, its exact ingredients are a matter of family preference, rather than adhering to any hard and fast rule. There is always flour and/or breadcrumbs, milk or water, and suet. Depending on the occasion and the budget there might also be spices, sugar, raisins, black treacle, golden syrup, grated apples, carrots and a splash of rum. The pudding is often served with double cream. Leftover pudding is sliced and fried with bacon and eggs for breakfast. Without the fruits and spices, it is a plain everyday suet pudding; with them, it is served for holidays, special occasions and 'daft days', the so-called days of merriment at Christmastime.[2]

Suet Pudding at School

Rib-sticking suet puddings were just the thing for active young students to fill up on. Accordingly, many English schools and colleges boasted their own special puddings. One of the earliest, Cambridge pudding, dates back to the seventeenth century and was a simple boiled suet pudding flavoured with dates and currants.

Steamed suet pudding is the basis for endless pudding variations, both sweet and savoury.

New College pudding, named after the Oxford college founded in 1379, is more unusual. The ingredients are typical – suet, flour or breadcrumbs, currants, lemon peel, sugar, nutmeg, eggs and occasionally brandy. The mixture was formed into small dumplings and fried, rather than being baked or steamed. A manuscript cookbook titled *Mrs Bescod's Book of Receipts – 1757* explained: 'Make the puddings in the shape of an egg & stew 'em in butter till they are of a fine brown colour and serve 'em up with Butter, Sugar & Sack.'

A nineteenth-century recipe from another Oxford college, Brasenose, was called 'Herodotus Pudding'. It was made with a pound of minced beef suet, breadcrumbs, raisins, figs, sugar, sherry and lemon peel, boiled for fourteen hours. Variations of the recipe appeared in many cookbooks of the era, both English and American, often prefaced by the note 'A Genuine Classical Receipt'. American cookbook author Jane Cunningham Croly added the comment:

> This receipt is really to be found in Herodotus. The only variations made in it are the substitution of sugar for honey, and sherry for the wine of ancient Greece. Half the quantity of suet would, we think, be an improvement, and half the time for boiling.[3]

A nearly identical pudding, called 'Figgy Pudding' rather than 'Herodotus', was traditionally served on Palm Sunday or at Christmastime. It inspired this verse of the song 'We Wish You a Merry Christmas':

> Oh, bring us a figgy pudding;
> Oh, bring us a figgy pudding;
> Oh, bring us a figgy pudding and a cup of good cheer.
> We won't go until we get some;
> We won't go until we get some;
> We won't go until we get some, so bring some out here.

5
Christmas Pudding

Life's a pudding full of plums.

W. S. Gilbert and Arthur Sullivan, *The Gondoliers*, 1889

Plum, or Christmas, pudding is the quintessence of suet pudding, its Platonic ideal. That is, the plum pudding we have come to know, seen depicted on Christmas cards and extolled by Bob Cratchit in yearly readings of *A Christmas Carol*. But it took many years to develop into the nineteenth-century festive pudding Dickens celebrated.

Plum pudding started out more modestly. In the sixteenth century it was a porridge made with meat, root vegetables and dried fruit, thickened with breadcrumbs. Over time and with the development of the pudding cloth, it became a more substantial pudding; for years, such puddings were served at the beginning of a meal. Gradually, the meat disappeared from the dish and it became a suet pudding with 'plums', which were in fact raisins plumped up in wine or brandy. In its plainest variation, it was the plum duff of the street sellers; in its richest, it was fit for royals and the stuff of nursery rhymes.

> When King Arthur first did reign
> He ruled like a king.

He bought three sacks of barley meal
To make a plum pudding.

The pudding it was made,
And duly stuffed with plums,
And lumps of suet put in it
As big as my two thumbs.

The king and queen sat down to it
And all the lords beside,
And what they couldn't eat that night,
The queen next morning fried.

By the mid-seventeenth century the richer plum pudding had become associated with Christmas feasting. However, in 1647 Oliver Cromwell and the Puritans banned Christmas observances and festive puddings, as they saw reflections of pagan festivals in traditions like the Yule log, and idol worship in nativity scenes. They were offended by the feasting and drunken revelry that took place on days that they thought should be spent in prayer and reflection. It wasn't until 1660, when Charles II took the throne, that the ban ended and the celebration of Christmas, complete with plum pudding, was restored.

Puddings in general gained status in the early eighteenth century, during the reign of George I, the 'Pudding King'. Later, with Queen Victoria's rule, Christmas became more festive and more family-oriented than ever. Victoria and German-born Prince Albert, like the reformed Ebenezer Scrooge, knew how to keep Christmas well. They feasted, exchanged gifts and encouraged their subjects to do the same, so far as they were able. In 1848 *The Illustrated London News* featured a woodcut of the royal family gathered around a Christmas tree, thus turning the German tradition into a holiday institution in England, and later in the United States. Plum pudding had moved to the dessert course long before and was served throughout the year, but it was essential to the Christmas celebration. Although it could be a relatively inexpensive dessert, English women who feared they wouldn't be able to afford even a small pudding at Christmastime joined pudding savings clubs and set aside their pennies until they had enough money to buy the necessary supplies.

Plum pudding at its most basic was a simple suet pudding made with breadcrumbs and/or flour, raisins and/or currants, brown sugar, suet, eggs, salt and cinnamon. A richer version

A wondrous pudding borne aloft by Father Christmas on the cover of a late 19th- or early 20th-century Christmas edition of *The Century*, illustration by Louis Rhead.

William Pitt and Napoleon help themselves to the world in James Gillray's 'The Plumb Pudding in Danger; or, State Epicures taking un Petit Soupe', 1805, hand-coloured etching.

might include such additions as candied fruit peel, almonds, apples, carrot, orange and lemon juice, nutmeg, mace and brandy. The pudding was usually served with a sauce, which might have been anything from a simple combination of confectioner's sugar and butter to a more complex one with brandy or rum added. The often-used term 'hard sauce' does not imply that the sauce is made with 'hard liquor'; rather it means that the sauce has the consistency of icing, rather than of a pourable sauce.

Pudding Lore and Legend

Dickens never used the phrase 'Christmas pudding' in *A Christmas Carol*, which was published in 1843. He simply wrote 'pudding'. He described it as a 'speckled cannon-ball, so hard

Advertisement for Atmore's Mincemeat, 1870–80. Note how the flames around the pudding mimic the curls around the gentleman's head.

and firm, blazing in half of half-a-quartern of ignited brandy, and bedight with Christmas holly stuck into the top'. It was a modest pudding, all the Cratchit family was able to manage on Bob Cratchit's meagre salary. Despite its small size Cratchit pronounced it 'a wonderful pudding!'; 'nobody said or thought it was at all a small pudding for a large family'. The first use of the name 'Christmas pudding' in print was in Anthony Trollope's novel *Doctor Thorne* (1858). In the book, sadly, the Reverend Caleb Oriel was said to have to eat his Christmas pudding alone.

Dickens spread the joys and generosity of the holiday, along with the serving of turkeys and plum pudding, far and wide. But he was not the only author to describe the pudding in glowing terms. In *The Mill on the Floss* (1860), George Eliot wrote:

> The plum-pudding was of the same handsome roundness as ever, and came in with the symbolic blue flames around it, as if it had been snatched from the nether fires into which it had been thrown by dyspeptic Puritans; the dessert was as splendid as ever, with its golden oranges, brown nuts, and the crystalline light and dark of apple-jelly and damson cheese: in all these things Christmas was as it had always been since Tom could remember.

Not all Christmas puddings turned out so splendid. In 1850, *The Illustrated London News* included a humorous story entitled 'The Dreadful Turn-Out of A French Plum-Pudding!', poking fun at the fact that all things English had become

Alfred Mills, 'The Pudding Bag', *c.* 1806, hand-coloured etching. When Cook doesn't know how to use a pudding bag, soup is the unhappy result.

fashionable in France. Its main characters were Monsieur and Madame de la Bêtise, 'Whose Grand Object in Life was to Live in the English Style'. In the story, the couple invited their friends to an English Christmas feast. The guests dressed as figures from English history, drank English beer, and ate '*rosbif*'. Madame de la Bêtise made a plum pudding, which she poured from a tea urn. The guests were dismayed by the soupy pudding and, fittingly enough, the gentleman dressed as Oliver Cromwell commanded the servant to 'take away the filthy stuff!' It seemed that Madame de la Bêtise had not realized that the pudding should be cooked in a cloth, and had merely boiled up all the ingredients in a pot of water.

The French chef Urbain Dubois included several pudding recipes in his cookbook, *Cuisine artistique* (1882). He prefaced his plum pudding recipe by sniffing that:

> The English Plum-Pudding is generally too heavy and massive: the one I am about to describe, which I always served up even at the most sumptuous dinners, is lighter and of a fine flavour.

He served his plum pudding aflame and accompanied by a 'boatful of sabayon or a frothy punch-sauce'. Despite his protestations to the contrary, the recipe is not notably different from those for most English plum puddings. Dubois was not alone in making such remarks. Even now, cookery writers often comment that the traditional plum pudding is too rich, too heavy and too indigestible and proceed to offer up their own new and improved versions, which are often neither new nor improved.

Too much of a good thing, in George Cruikshank's 'Indigestion', 1835, etching.

Rituals and Superstitions

The great English Christmas pudding is as rich with ritual as it is with spices and fruits. Since it usually contains some brandy or rum, it can be kept for a long time and may be made up to a year before the holiday. But one of the many customs that have arisen around the pudding calls for it to be made about a month before Christmas, during the week following Stir-up Sunday. This is the last Sunday before the season of Advent, the time of preparation for Christmas, and is so called because on that Sunday in Anglican churches the collect in the Book of Common Prayer of 1549 begins:

> Stir up, we beseech thee, O Lord, the wills of thy faithful people; that they, plenteously bringing forth the fruit of good works, may of thee be plenteously rewarded.

Kenny Meadows, 'Taking Up the Christmas Pudding', from *The Illustrated London News*, 1848. Making the Christmas pudding was a family affair in 19th-century London.

When the pudding is being stirred up, everyone in the household is supposed to take a turn stirring it and, while doing so, to make a wish. Some believe that the pudding should be made with thirteen ingredients, to represent the twelve Apostles and Jesus. Before the pudding is steamed charms or coins are tucked into it; one of the charms is typically a ring, which may account for this popular riddle:

> Flour of England, fruit of Spain
> Met together in a shower of rain;
> Put in a bag, tied round with a string
> If you'll tell me this riddle,
> I'll give you a ring.

The answer, of course, is a plum pudding.

After it is steamed, the pudding is stored away to mellow until Christmas Day, when it is reheated and then topped with a sprig of holly. Some people say the holly represents Christ's crown of thorns, while others think the custom goes back to pagan tradition, in which holly was believed to keep witches away. Just before the pudding is served it is doused with brandy, set alight and triumphantly borne to the table wreathed in blue flames. When the pudding was served in Agatha Christie's tale 'The Adventure of the Christmas Pudding', Hercule Poirot found a silver bachelor's button in his slice, indicating that he would remain a bachelor at least for another year. Another guest found a ring, meaning marriage was in her future; still another found a thimble, indicating that for her it was not. When Colonel Lacey found a chunk of red glass in his slice, Poirot realized it was the stolen ruby and the key to solving the crime.

THERE'S PLENTY OF ROOM AT THE TABLE. WHY NOT ASK THE HUNGRY
LITTLE FELLOW TO SIT DOWN?

Will Uncle Sam share the prosperity plum pudding with Cuba, Puerto
Rico and the Philippines? Emil Flohri's cover of *Judge*, 3 February 1906.

Plum Pudding in America

Dickens taught America what Christmas dinner should consist of, but plum pudding never became as iconic in the US as it was in England. In the nineteenth century, pudding rituals were not as commonly observed, and the pudding was as apt to be served on the Thanksgiving table as on the Christmas one. The cookery author Sarah Josepha Hale, who was a moving force in making Thanksgiving a national holiday and a way to bring the nation together after the Civil War, was not enthusiastic about plum puddings. She gave her grudging approval to serving them at Christmastime, writing:

> As Christmas comes but once a year, a rich plum pudding may be permitted for the feast, though it is not healthy food; and children should be helped very sparingly . . . In cold weather, there is less danger of injury from mince pies and plum puddings; still for the sedentary, the delicate, or dyspeptic they are never safe.[1]

Many other nineteenth-century American writers lacked enthusiasm for plum pudding. Eliza Leslie included it as part of her recommended Christmas menu, but wrote that flaming it was 'always foolish'. Recipes were more often titled 'Plum Pudding' than 'Christmas Pudding' and cookbooks offered versions of differing richness. Some were quite meagre, containing only raisins for fruit and the smallest pinch of spice. Some recipes omitted alcohol in deference to the growing Temperance movement; one, in fact, recommended grape juice rather than rum or brandy in the pudding's sauce.[2]

In the mid-twentieth century, if it was served at all, the plum pudding was likely to be tinned. Desserts in Christmas colours became fashionable in the US, with cherry angel food

Americans celebrated Thanksgiving with plum pudding, as shown on this postcard of 1908.

cake layered with lime gelatin being a typical example. The nadir was reached in 1942 with the *Good Housekeeping Cook Book*'s 'White Christmas Pudding'. Made with gelatin, canned pineapple juice, coconut, frozen strawberries and whipped cream, it bore no relationship to any pudding Tiny Tim would have recognized.

6

Hasty Pudding

The sweets of Hasty Pudding.
Joel Barlow, 'The Hasty Pudding', 1793

Joel Barlow loved hasty pudding. In 1793, when he was living in France and feeling homesick for New England and his favourite foods, someone served him a dish of it. He was so transported by its familiar taste that he wrote an ode to it:

> I sing the sweets I know, the charms I feel,
> My morning incense, and my evening meal,
> The sweets of Hasty Pudding.
> . . .
> Dear Hasty Pudding, what unpromised joy
> Expands my heart, to meet thee in Savoy!
> Doomed o'er the world through devious paths to roam,
> Each clime my country, and each house my home,
> My soul is soothed, my cares have found an end,
> I greet my long-lost, unforgotten friend.

Today, despite his many other accomplishments as a diplomat and writer, Barlow's poem to the humble pudding is his best-known work. Written in mock epic style, the nearly 3,000-word poem is as grandiose as the pudding it exalts is plain. The only ingredients mentioned in the poem are cornmeal, salt, milk and molasses. No cinnamon, cloves or nutmeg enhanced its flavour, no raisins, currants or apples enlivened it. Barlow called it hasty pudding, but it also was known as Indian pudding, since it was made with cornmeal or, as he wrote, 'powdered gold'. Indian pudding was not so called because Native Americans made it, but because they taught the settlers how to grow the corn, or maize, which was a New World crop.

In 1795, two years after Barlow wrote 'The Hasty Pudding', some students at Harvard established a secret club to 'cultivate the social affections and cherish the feelings of friendship and patriotism'. The undergraduates named the organization the Hasty Pudding Club and required that its members 'provide a pot of hasty pudding for every meeting'.

A pudding-eating contest depicted in 'The Humors of a Country Wake', 1794, hand-coloured etching.

Oddly, Joel Barlow was a graduate of Harvard's arch-rival Yale. The club's pudding ritual was discontinued in the early 1800s. Today, the Hasty Pudding Club is known for its annual theatrical performances rather than its puddings and the tradition lives on only in its famed pudding pots. Every year, club members select two prominent showbusiness personalities as man and woman of the year. As part of the festivities, they are each presented with a golden pudding pot. It is unlikely that any of the pots have ever contained a pudding.

Porridge to pudding

The origins of hasty pudding go back to the Middle Ages when gruels or porridges of flour or oats mixed with milk or water were cooked in a pot over a fire. In the seventeenth century they were named 'Pudding in Haste' or 'Hasty Pudding' because they were not boiled for hours like black and other puddings. As the playwright Thomas Heywood wrote in *The English Traveller* (1633), a hasty pudding was 'longer in eating than it was in making'.[1] Robert May included three hasty pudding recipes, all made with flour, in *The Accomplisht Cook* (1660). The first added milk or cream, 'raisins of the sun', currants, butter, grated bread and nutmeg to the flour, to be boiled for a quarter of an hour. May suggested dishing it up on beaten butter. His second hasty pudding was unusual in that it was boiled in a bag and contained sugar, which the first did not. He wrote, 'If it be well made, it will be as good as a Custard.' May's third pudding was stirred, but it was richer since it was made with six egg yolks in addition to the ingredients of the first. He served it elegantly, with thinly sliced preserved orange peel, beaten butter and sugar.

Despite May's hasty pudding in a bag, the typical hasty pudding was stirred in a pot for a short time. The puddings had to be stirred continuously to keep the mixture smooth and to prevent it from sticking to the pot and burning. Some recipes mentioned the need to stir in only one direction to prevent lumps from forming. During the eighteenth century, Hannah Glasse made hasty puddings with flour and also with oatmeal. Oatmeal-based hasty puddings were common in the North of England and in Scotland; Glasse's called for nothing but water, butter, salt and oatmeal. She said it was 'best made with Scotch oatmeal' and suggested eating the pudding 'with wine and sugar, or ale and sugar, or cream, or new milk'. She flavoured one of her flour-based hasty puddings with bay leaves and included two egg yolks in the recipe. She wrote: 'you may omit the egg if you do not like it; but it is a great addition to the pudding; and a little piece of butter stirred in the milk makes it eat short and fine'. The puddings were typically served hot.

Hasty Pudding in America

Early American settlers lacked flour and sugar for their hasty puddings, so they did what cooks always do: they used the ingredients at hand to make something resembling what they knew. In place of flour, they used cornmeal; in place of sugar, molasses.

American Cookery, written by Amelia Simmons and published in 1796, was the first cookbook written and published in the United States. Among its uniquely American recipes were three for Indian pudding, which were all printed under the single heading 'A Nice Indian Pudding'. Each one was made with cornmeal and milk. Simmons added eggs, raisins, butter, spice and sugar to the first recipe and baked it for one-and-a-half hours. The second was baked for two-and-a-half-hours and called for either sugar or molasses. Simmons didn't specify sugar or molasses for the final version; she simply said 'sweeten'. This one was boiled in a cloth or pot for twelve hours.

Despite the fact that cornmeal required a much longer cooking time than flour, the word 'hasty' was used to describe the pudding as frequently as 'Indian'. No matter what they called it, Americans loved the dish. When President John Adams was a Harvard student, daily fare at the college generally consisted of beef, mutton and Indian pudding. Long afterwards, in retirement, he and his wife Abigail still began their Sunday dinners with Indian pudding. Abigail's cousin Josiah Quincy later wrote that the pudding was intended to fill up young boys like himself so that they would have less room for the meat that followed.[2]

Hasty pudding was so well recognized in America that the phrase 'thick as hasty pudding' was used in recipes for other dishes as an indication of the desired consistency. It was also used as a simile as in the Revolutionary War-era song 'Yankee Doodle':

Yankee Doodle went to town
A-riding on a pony
Stuck a feather in his hat
And called it macaroni.
. . .
Father and I went down to camp
Along with Captain Gooding
And there we saw the men and boys
As thick as hasty pudding.

Hasty or Indian pudding became a symbol of American independence, a dish that was enjoyed by every class, everywhere from New England to Virginia, from New York to Pennsylvania. So it's surprising that Benjamin Thompson (later known as Count Rumford), an American who was born in 1753 and fled to England during the Revolution, later recommended hasty pudding to the English. Thompson, famed for his many inventions and innovations including a portable field kitchen and a coffee percolator, was admitted to the Royal Society in England in 1781. Later, he was named a Count of the Holy Roman Empire for his services to Bavaria. He took the name Rumford for the town in New Hampshire where he once taught.

Rumford's collected writings include an essay in which he proposed that hasty pudding be used an economical food for the poor. Despite the fact that the English had been making hasty pudding for hundreds of years, albeit with different grains, he defined the pudding and described its making in meticulous detail. He explained how to make a basic stirred pudding and one boiled in a bag, noted that dried apples and other fruits could be added to the pudding, and described Italian polenta as a similar dish. To serve the pudding, he recommended spreading it on a plate while it was still hot, then making an 'excavation' in its middle:

Into which excavation a piece of butter as large as a nutmeg is put, and upon it a spoonful of brown sugar, or more commonly of molasses. The butter being soon melted by the heat of the pudding mixes with the sugar or molasses, and forms a sauce, which, being confined in the excavation made for it, occupies the middle of the plate. The pudding is then eaten with a spoon, each spoonful of it being dipped into the sauce before it is carried to the mouth; care being had, in taking it up, to begin on the outside or near the brim of the plate, and to approach the centre by regular advances, in order not to demolish too soon the excavation which forms the reservoir for the sauce.[3]

Apparently, Rumford's advice was not followed. Few recipes for hasty pudding were included in nineteenth-century English cookbooks. Eliza Acton had none; nor did Isabella Beeton. She merely wrote:

The porridge of the Scotch is nothing more than a species of hasty pudding, composed of oatmeal, salt, and water; and the 'red pottage' for which Esau sold his birthright, must have been something similar.[4]

Although the name 'hasty' died out in England, simple stirred puddings continued to be popular. They were generally named after the main ingredient, which might be semolina, tapioca, sago, flour or oatmeal, but not cornmeal. These puddings were categorized as 'nursery puddings' or 'milk puddings' since milk was almost always among their ingredients, and their simplicity made them perfect nursery food.

Indian Pudding for Dessert

By the nineteenth century, America's Indian pudding had moved to the end of the meal, and its ingredients usually included raisins and other fruits. Apples were a popular addition and, according to one manuscript cookbook, they 'afford an exceedingly rich jelly' in the pudding. Also called 'Yankee' pudding, Indian puddings were usually stirred on the stovetop until smooth, then baked for a few hours before being served warm, often with cream or a molasses sauce. Some recipes called for the pudding to be baked in a 'bean-pot'. Some, but certainly not all, of the recipes added spices such as ginger, cinnamon and nutmeg to the puddings. Occasionally rice or tapioca puddings with some cornmeal added would be named 'Indian Tapioca Pudding', or 'Indian Rice Pudding'. Once in a while, a recipe would be titled 'Indian' despite its lack of any cornmeal at all. Naturally enough, the 1918 edition of Fannie Farmer's *The Boston Cooking-School Cook Book* did include a traditional Indian pudding recipe, but Farmer also offered a recipe for a 'Mock Indian Pudding'. Like similar recipes in other books, the pudding was made with buttered 'baker's entire-wheat bread', molasses and milk and baked for two to three hours. The pudding may have been 'mock', but it was neither Indian nor hasty.

7
Bread Pudding

Hurrah for puddin'-owning.
Norman Lindsay, *The Magic Pudding*, 2006

Bread pudding, usually thought of as a thrifty way to turn stale bread into an economical dessert, started out as a rather more elegant and expensive dish. The fourteenth-century French household guide *Le Ménagier de Paris* included directions for making a version called a *taillis*. A Lenten variety was made with bread and biscuits combined with raisins, apples, almond milk, saffron and sugar. It was not cooked: hot almond milk was simply poured over the bread and other ingredients and the mixture was left to set.[1]

By the seventeenth century, an English dish called a white-pot was being made with 'fine' (good-quality) bread, rich cream, eggs and spices. White-pots were distinguished by being baked instead of boiled in a bag like most puddings of their day. A Devonshire white-pot was so called because Devonshire was a dairy farming county known for its excellent cream. A typical white-pot recipe, from *The Compleat Cook* by Nathaniel Brook published in 1658, called for 'a penny Loaf of fine bread sliced very thin' along with cream, eggs, nutmeg, sugar, butter, salt and 'a handfull of Raisins of the Sun'.

Robert May had a similar recipe in the 1685 edition of *The Accomplisht Cook* but he added 'pippins' (a variety of apple) boiled to 'pap'. May directed the cook to 'cut some sippets [bread cut into small pieces] very thin and dry them before the fire'. When the sippets and pippins were ready, he layered them in a pan, poured on the cream mixture and baked it.

Bread and Batter

In Hannah Glasse's day, bread puddings were more apt to be a humble family dessert, a thrifty way to use up stale bread and crumbs. In fact, a recipe for French bread in an eighteenth-century manuscript cookbook concluded by saying the 'chipping', or broken pieces, could be used to make a good pudding.

Many bread puddings were made by soaking stale bread to make a batter instead of layering slices of bread with other ingredients. The bread was steeped in milk or cream, or even in water, and then beaten up with whatever other ingredients were being used. The resulting batter was boiled in a pudding cloth or poured into a pudding dish, covered and steamed. Glasse added almonds, rose water and wine to one such pudding, which she called a 'fine Bread Pudding'. Her 'ordinary Bread Pudding' called for milk rather than cream, fewer eggs and no wine, although she did suggest adding a little ginger. By contrast, Glasse's 'Puddings for little Dishes' were much more fanciful than most bread puddings. The recipe called for a batter made with a combination of bread, cream, nutmeg, sugar and eggs, beaten together. This was to be divided among five wooden pudding dishes, with one portion coloured yellow with saffron, one red with cochineal, another green with spinach juice, another blue with the syrup of violets and the

Is there anything more comforting than an old-fashioned bread and butter pudding?

final, largest portion to be mixed with almonds to remain white. The puddings were to be boiled for an hour, then turned out onto a serving dish with the white pudding in the middle and the four coloured ones surrounding it. Before serving them, Glasse recommended topping them with melted butter, wine and sugar.

Isabella Beeton's nineteenth-century recipe for a 'Very Plain Bread Pudding' required the bread to be soaked in water rather than milk or cream. However, she wrote that milk would 'very much improve' it. Batter-style bread puddings were also frequently made with breadcrumbs rather than with soaked and beaten bread. They could be rich or meagre according to the cook's ways and means. Eliza Acton called a simple bread pudding 'The Poor Author's Pudding'. She wittily titled a much more elaborate one 'The Publisher's Pudding', and wrote that it could 'scarcely be made too rich'.

Poignant Puddings

The most meagre bread puddings were neither batter- nor layer-style. Made in Britain and America, they were simply small loaves of bread, boiled or steamed and served with a simple sauce. Glasse made one she called a 'boiled Loaf', which consisted of a small loaf of bread with a half pint of boiling milk poured over it. It was tied up in a cloth and boiled, and then turned onto a dish. It was cooked for only half an

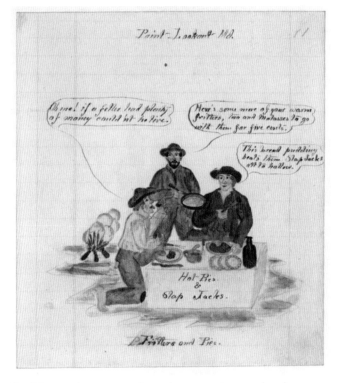

Confederate prisoners appreciate a chance to enjoy some bread pudding in John Jacob Omenhausser's 'Fritters and Pies', c. 1864, ink and watercolour.

hour because the shape of the loaf needed to be retained. The boiled loaf was served with melted butter and had wine or rose water poured over it, and sugar sprinkled on top. The pudding must have been commonly made since Glasse wrote that 'there are little loaves made on purpose for the use'.

In 1882, Susan Anna Brown's *The Book of Forty Puddings* included a sad little 'Simple Pudding'. It consisted of nothing more than a small loaf of bread with the crust cut off, folded in a napkin and steamed. Brown recommended serving it with a sauce made with butter, cream and sugar.

Sandwich-style Puddings

Mrs A.D.T. Whitney, a nineteenth-century cookbook author, called her bread puddings 'sandwich puddings'. She explained:

> By these I mean puddings of fruit and bread, either in slices or crumbs, made in layers, and baked. They are all after the same plan, and like every other class of dishes may, when understood as a class, be varied and multiplied according to one's own pleasure and ingenuity.[2]

Bread puddings made in the sandwich style became more prevalent as time went on and nearly every cookbook in Britain and America had recipes for them. Generally they were made, as Whitney wrote, 'after the same plan'. Slices of firm or stale bread, either plain, buttered or jam-covered, were layered in a pan with currants, apples or other fruit between the layers. Then cream, milk or custard was poured over the bread and the pudding was left to soak for a time before baking. Toasted breadcrumbs or cubes of bread might take the place of sliced bread.

Cinnamon, ginger, nutmeg, mace, bay leaves, fresh or candied lemon peel, raisins, currants, brandy, sherry, rose water, apples, cherries, coconut, cocoa, marmalade and jam were all additions to the basic recipe at one time or another. The bread itself varied; as well as white bread, brown bread was also used, and some thrifty cooks made bread pudding using slices of leftover plum pudding. During the nineteenth and twentieth centuries, biscuits, stale cake, brioche, challah, soda crackers, shredded wheat biscuits, popcorn and matzo all stood in for bread. Savoury ingredients including cheese, onions, herbs, bacon, ham and fish were mixed into bread puddings intended to be served as a side dish, a simple supper or for breakfast. Today, when bread pudding is served for breakfast, it is often called 'baked French toast', or 'breakfast strata', rather than pudding.

Sunday Best Puddings

At the opposite end of the spectrum from homey bread puddings were elegant, 'Sunday best' bread puddings. Queen's pudding, named for Victoria, was baked using a mixture of breadcrumbs and milk or custard. It was then covered with a tart jelly, usually currant, and topped with meringue before being baked again just long enough to turn the meringue to gold. Apple Charlotte, another elegant bread pudding, was made in a mould lined with buttered – and often previously fried – slices of bread and filled with cooked, sweetened apples and bread or cake crumbs, then baked. It is thought to have been named for Queen Charlotte (1744–1818), wife of George III and a patron of apple growers. In Russia, a similar dessert was known as a *sharlotka*, and was made with breadcrumbs, wine, apples and raisins. Charlotte Russe, an unbaked pudding, featured ladyfingers in place of the bread slices, and the centre was filled with a lush cream filling and glacé fruit. It was created by the famed French chef Marie-Antoine Carême early in the nineteenth century.

One of the most elaborate bread puddings was called either a 'diplomat' or 'cabinet' pudding, perfect for serving

Queen of puddings. This elegant pudding is said to have been a favourite of Queen Victoria.

when high-ranking guests came to call. Sponge cake, lady-fingers, macaroons or some combination of the three took the place of bread, and they were layered with candied fruits. A rich custard was poured over this and the pudding was either baked or steamed. An uncooked version could be made by adding some gelatin to the custard. Often, gilding the lily somewhat, the pudding was served with a sauce or heavy cream. Trifle, a close relative of cabinet pudding, includes layers of cake and boiled custard and is not baked. Queen of puddings, another dressed-up bread pudding, is baked, topped with jam or preserves and meringue, then baked a second time to brown the meringue.

Summer Pudding

Today, summer pudding is one of Britain's most delightful desserts, and one that has proven fit for a queen. A June 1982 dinner menu for Queen Elizabeth II featured summer pudding for dessert. It was the only menu item written in English rather than French.[3]

To make a summer pudding, fresh berries are cooked with a little sugar just long enough for the sugar to melt. Alternatively, the berries and sugar are simply stirred together until the grains dissolve, without heating. Either way, the mixture is poured into a pudding mould or bowl lined with slightly stale bread. The mould is topped with another layer of bread, then chilled with a weight on top to compact the pudding. When the pudding is turned out onto a serving dish, the bread has been transformed into a beautiful shade of red, blue or violet depending on the fruit used, and the result is a colourful, light summery pud. It is served alone or with cream.

Summer pudding, one of the splendid delights of the season.

Summer pudding aficionados often have a firm preference as to which berries are best, but all sorts have been used – fresh redcurrants, raspberries, gooseberries, blueberries and more. The Queen's was not specified on the menu. The origins of summer pudding are debated. Since it was sometimes called 'hydropathic pudding', it may have originated at health resorts where one took the waters in the nineteenth century, for the pudding was considered less rich and more digestible than most pastries. The more appealing name, 'summer pudding', began to be used around the turn of the twentieth century. Similar puddings have been called Malvern, Rhode Island, Wakefield and berry pudding. In America, Maria Parloa's book *Miss Parloa's New Cook Book* (1880) had a recipe for a summer pudding she called 'black pudding'. It was made with blueberries.

In Other Lands

Most countries that eat bread have some form of bread pudding and every cook has their own variation on the theme. The *torta Nicolotta* of Venice combines cubes of bread with the crusts removed with a custard sauce flavoured with rum-soaked raisins, candied citron, vanilla and cinnamon. It is baked and served at room temperature or cooled.

An Egyptian bread pudding called *om Ali*, 'Ali's mother', is made with either bread or broken pieces of phyllo pastry along with milk or cream, raisins and almonds. According to one of the myths associated with the pudding, it was invented by a poor villager to feed a sultan who happened to be passing through the town. Her creation not only won his praise but became – and remains – an Egyptian favourite.

Shahi tukra, from India, is made with bread that has been fried in ghee (clarified butter) and is flavoured with cardamom, raisins and nuts. A bread pudding from the Jewish community in Calcutta, *apam*, is thought to have been influenced by bread pudding cooked during the British Raj. However, it's made with coconut milk so that the pudding may be eaten after meat, since Jewish tradition prohibits eating dairy products with or soon after meat.

Mexico's *capirotada* is an unusual Easter-time bread pudding. It is meatless so it is appropriate for Lenten meals, but since it is so festive it is often served for Easter as well. Rather than custard or milk, the bread is soaked and baked in a syrup made with water, brown sugar, cinnamon and cloves. It can also contain an assortment of other ingredients that may include strong cheese, peanuts, raisins and apples. 'All this, and those things people will not tell you', writes Alberto Alvaro Ríos in *Capirotada: A Nogales Memoir*. He calls it 'a food piñata'.[4]

From ancient times to today, from England to Egypt, bread puddings have been popular with everyone from commoners to queens. Jane Austen's mother, Cassandra, thought her bread pudding good enough to serve to a vicar. Since she herself was married to a parish priest, she would have been a good judge of the dish's appropriateness. She set out the recipe in the form of a poem, entitled 'A Receipt for a Pudding' (1808). The first verse reads:

> If the Vicar you treat,
> You must give him to eat,
> A pudding to hit his affection;
> And to make his repast,
> By the canon of taste,
> Be the present receipt your direction.

8

Rice Pudding

It's lovely rice pudding for dinner again!
A. A. Milne, *When We Were Very Young*, 1924

Creamy rice pudding spiced with cinnamon and plump raisins is a real treat. But plain rice pudding served again and again as a nursery dinner is enough to make anyone cry, as A. A. Milne knew so well. His poem 'Rice Pudding' asks what the matter is with Mary Jane:

> She's crying with all her might and main,
> And she won't eat her dinner – rice pudding again –
> What *is* the matter with Mary Jane?

The poem continues for four more stanzas and despite offers of a doll, sweets and even a train ride, Mary Jane cannot stop crying over her rice pudding. In the 1920s, when Milne wrote his poem, rice pudding was a regular nursery meal and was usually served completely plain. Rice was soft, bland and easy to digest, so the dish was considered appropriate for children and the sick. The pudding was often nothing more than rice boiled in milk or water; it lacked sugar, spice, eggs or butter. It might be served with a sugary sauce, but otherwise

This is a rice pudding Mary Jane would probably love to have *again*.

it was boring and rather tasteless. However, warm, milky rice pudding became the stuff of fond childhood memories for some, occupying a special place that has much to do with nostalgia and little to do with flavour.

Rice from East to West

Rice was a staple food throughout Asia for centuries before it arrived in the West. In fact, rice pudding is said to be the first food the Buddha ate when he decided to break his fast and renounce extreme deprivation as the path to enlightenment. However, rice was still a rare and precious import when Elizabeth I ruled England. Those who could afford it kept it securely locked up in their spice cabinets and used it sparingly.

One of the earliest recipes specifically for 'A Ryce Pudding' was in John Murrell's *A New Booke of Cookerie*, published in 1615. Murrell steeped rice in milk overnight, then drained it and combined it with minced beef, currants, eggs, nutmeg, cinnamon, sugar and barberries. He stuffed the mixture into guts and boiled it. The same year, Gervase Markham, author of *The English Hus-Wife*, recommended that rice be boiled in 'the best, sweetest and thickest Cream'. This should have added to it egg yolks, dates, spices and suet, and be boiled it in 'forms', which were shallow pudding moulds. The pudding should be served when it is a day old.[1]

By the beginning of the eighteenth century, rice became more available as the American colonies supplied England with large quantities of prized Carolina rice. Although that source ended temporarily during the American Revolution, when trade resumed rice became more affordable. As it did, rice puddings became more common. Hannah Glasse had several recipes in the 1796 edition of her cookbook, including a 'Carolina Rice Pudding'. Some of her rice puddings were rich with eggs, spices, butter and fruit. Others, labelled 'cheap', lacked eggs and, except for raisins, fruit. A few were still boiled in a pudding bag, but most recipes called for the rice to be cooked in milk, then mixed with the other ingredients and baked, often in pans lined with puff pastry.

Although recipes for Indian-style 'pellaw' appeared in various cookbooks, the customary way to serve rice in nineteenth-century Britain was as pudding. Mrs Beeton wrote: 'Baking it in puddings is the best mode of preparing it.' Accordingly, she had nearly a dozen rice pudding recipes in her book, many designated for the nursery. She called them 'Plain and Economical; a nice Pudding for Children' and 'a nice dish for the Nursery'. Eliza Acton also described one of her many rice pudding recipes as 'Cheap Rice Pudding' and a 'nice dish for the nursery'; however, she also offered more appealing puddings including one titled 'Normandy Pudding. (Good.)'. It was made by layering rice pudding with sweetened redcurrants or Kentish cherries in a tart pan and baking it.

In the late nineteenth and early twentieth centuries, cooks had fun with rice pudding. They moulded the pudding in teacups, making a cavity in the centre and filling it with brightly coloured jelly; they layered individual rice puddings with cooked fruit; they folded custard sauce or stiffly beaten egg whites into rice puddings before baking them; some topped puddings with meringue. They also made 'snow-balls': Acton, for example, coated peeled whole apples or oranges with a layer of cooked rice. Then she wrapped each one in a pudding cloth and boiled it for an hour or so, depending on the size of the fruit. She served her snow-balls sprinkled with sugar or with a mixture of butter, sugar and cinnamon or nutmeg. Estelle Woods Wilcox's *Buckeye Cookery* included a different rice snow-ball recipe. It called for plain boiled rice to be moulded into balls and arranged on a dish, and for lemon custard sauce to be poured over them half an hour before serving. The recipe was contributed by a Miss Louise Skinner, who said it made 'a very simple but nice dessert'.

Cooking Methods

Some nineteenth-century cooks made rice pudding by steeping the rice overnight in milk, cream or water, then draining it, just as Markham, Murrell and others had done. But then, rather than boiling the pudding in a bag, they simmered it on a stovetop with fresh milk or cream along with sugar, raisins, spices and often eggs. By that time, meat and suet were long gone from rice puddings. In an early twentieth-century manuscript cookbook, an Englishwoman named Mrs Metcalfe suggested an efficient approach to timing the cooking of a pudding made with a combination of rice and tapioca. She wrote:

> At 9 A.M. Put one tablespoonful of Carolina rice and one tablespoonful tapioca into a 3 pint pie dish; add 1 tablespoonful coarse brown sugar & a small pinch of salt. Let this soak on the hob, or close to the fire until eleven o'clock & let it be constantly stirred. Then put very little pats of butter on this, & put it in a moderate oven. For the first half hour, stir it often from the bottom, then leave it. By one o'clock, you will have a pudding far exceeding in richness one made with eggs & with a delicious flavour. Rice or tapioca alone are equally good.

Although the pudding was titled 'Milk pudding without eggs', she never mentioned the milk, which must have been mixed with the rice and tapioca at the outset.

Other rice pudding recipes omitted the pre-soaking and called instead for uncooked rice to be mixed with the other ingredients and simmered until the rice became soft and creamy. Uncooked rice might also be combined with the other ingredients, then baked in a slow oven for up to three hours, while other cooks began with previously cooked rice, added the other ingredients, and either boiled or baked the mixture. When rice puddings are baked, a brown crust forms on the top. It is either completely inedible or the best part of the pudding, depending on the person describing it.

Chefs' Rice Pudding

Rice pudding is nothing if not versatile. It's a blank canvas to which cooks can bring their own artistry. In the hands of nineteenth-century French chefs, rice pudding soared to new heights of sophistication. *Riz à l'impératrice*, rice pudding fit for an empress, was rich with candied fruits, liqueurs, custard and whipped cream. It was moulded, chilled and topped with more candied fruits or syrup. Marcel Proust and M.F.K. Fisher were among its fans. *Poires condé*, another chilled French version, was made up of layers of rice pudding baked with sliced pears, and then topped with a pear and brandy sauce. The chef Urbain Dubois carried away the prize for panache with a rice pudding moulded in the shape of a pineapple, glazed with apricot marmalade and crowned with angelica to replicate a pineapple's leafy crown. Dubois wrote that done properly, it was sure to 'meet with applause'.[2]

In America, Rufus Estes, a former slave who became a chef, described a more down-to-earth but impressive cocoa rice meringue pudding in his book, *Good Things to Eat*, published in 1911. His dish mixed cocoa and raisins with the rice and milk; this was cooked, then cooled and had stiffly beaten egg whites and whipped cream folded in. The mixture was poured into a baking dish, topped with more egg whites mixed with cocoa and sugar, and baked until the meringue was golden brown.

Around the World

Rice puddings were and are varied around the globe. *Milchreis*, a German rice pudding, is made by cooking rice on the stove-top in milk with sugar and vanilla. It is usually served with fruit or topped with sugar and cinnamon. Bulgarian rice pudding is flavoured with lemon and garnished with pistachios and rose petals.

In Iran, *sholeh zard* is flavoured with saffron, almonds and rose water; a similar version is made in Afghanistan. *Firni*, popular throughout the Middle East, is flavoured similarly but is made with rice flour, rather than grains of rice. Latin Americans spice their *arróz con leche* with cinnamon, vanilla and raisins soaked in tequila. North Americans use the same flavours, minus the tequila. *Kheer*, a slow-cooked Indian rice pudding, includes raisins, cardamom, cinnamon, almonds,

On the most special occasions, *kheer*, a traditional South Asian rice pudding, may be topped with silver or gold leaf.

pistachios and saffron. It is sometimes decorated with silver or gold leaf. The Chinese make a steamed rice pudding with eight varieties of preserved fruit because Confucius believed eight was the number of perfection. In Southeast Asia, the rice may be black and the milk may be coconut.

In some countries, rice pudding gets all dressed up for holidays and celebrations.

On such occasions, the Portuguese decorate the top of their rice pudding, *arróz doce*, with festive swirls and symbols in powdered cinnamon. In Denmark at Christmastime, it's customary to serve a rice pudding called *risalamande* (the name is a variation of the French *riz à l'amande*). A whole almond is hidden in the pudding, and whoever finds it gets a prize, traditionally a marzipan pig. Sweden has a similar tradition, but the person who finds the almond is destined to be married within a year.

In Turkey, rice pudding, or *zerde*, is flavoured with saffron and rose water and customarily served at weddings. But the country's most famous and ancient pudding, according to legend, is *asure* or Noah's pudding. The pudding defies easy categorization since it's made with small amounts of many ingredients including, but not limited to, rice, wheat, white beans, chickpeas, sugar, apricots, figs, raisins, chestnuts, orange peel and rose water. The wheat, beans and chickpeas are soaked overnight and then simmered in water until tender; then the other ingredients are stirred into the pudding and it's cooked some more. It is served cooled and garnished with more fruits and nuts. The pudding's name is from *Asure Günü*, the Arabic for the Day of Ashura, the tenth day of Muharram, the first month of the Muslim calendar. According to legend, on that date Noah and his family reached land and were able to leave the ark. To celebrate, they made a pudding from what little was left of their provisions – some grains of rice, a few

Saffron, pistachio and coconut add sophisticated flavour to rice pudding.

A typical Spanish dessert, *arroz con leche* or rice with milk, sprinkled with cinnamon.

beans, a handful of chickpeas, some fruits and a few nuts. Today's more bountiful *asure* is often served during the holy month; a symbol of hospitality and generosity, the pudding is shared with relatives, friends and neighbours.

9
Batter Pudding

Hail bounteous Pudding! hot or cold, all hail!
William Woty (pen name Jemmy Copywell), 'Pudding', 1759

The pairing of roast beef and Yorkshire pudding is one of the great culinary marriages of all time. It was the classic British Sunday lunch for generations and is still esteemed and enjoyed today. Although the residents of the Yorkshire region claim the pudding as their own unique dish, one only they can make perfectly, it is made and celebrated all over the world.

The first printed recipe for what we now call Yorkshire pudding was published in 1737 in an anonymously written book, *The Whole Duty of a Woman*. It was called 'A Dripping Pudding' and was partnered with a shoulder of mutton, not roast beef. Ten years later, Hannah Glasse published her version in *The Art of Cookery Made Plain and Easy* and called it 'Yorkshire Pudding'. She did not specify the type of meat she cooked with it. Both authors compared the batter for the pudding to pancake batter: the earlier recipe instructed the reader to 'Make a good batter as for pancakes', while Glasse's recipe was more explicit. She called for a quart (1 l) of milk, four eggs, a little salt and sufficient flour to make a batter. Both authors emphasized that the batter had to be poured into a very hot pan.

At the time, meat was generally roasted on a spit before the fire, and a pan was placed several inches below the meat to catch the drippings. To make a Yorkshire pudding, the batter would be poured into the sizzling-hot dripping pan shortly before the meat was done so that the pudding would absorb the juices and flavour of the meat above it. The bottom of the pudding would become crisp and the top surface would swell up. Pouring the batter into a very hot pan is key to producing a light, airy pudding with a crisp crust. Some cooks flipped the pudding over to give the top a crust as well. When ovens became more common than open fires, many cooks roasted the meat on a rack with a dripping pan below to get the same meaty flavour into the pudding. Oddly enough, some recipes failed to specify that the pan should be hot. Even Mrs Beeton got it wrong. She said that the pudding should be put in the oven for an hour, then placed under the meat 'to catch a little of the gravy that flows from it'. Yorkshire natives claimed this as proof that no one but a Northerner could make a proper Yorkshire pudding.

When cooked sausages are added to Yorkshire pudding batter, the resulting pudding is called toad-in-the-hole.

Breakfast Puffs and Pop-overs

The traditional Yorkshire pudding was made in one piece the size of the dripping pan, then cut into squares and served. Yorkshire pudding was made the same way in America. Then, in 1877, American cousins to Yorkshire pudding popped up in a cookbook by Mary Foote Henderson titled *Practical Cooking and Dinner Giving*. Called 'Breakfast Puffs, or Pop-overs', they were small, individual puddings made like Yorkshire pudding with a flour, milk and egg batter. However, since

Today, individual Yorkshire puddings are popular.

they were not made with meat drippings, the flavour was quite different.[1] Again, the key to success was starting with piping hot pans. Later, Fannie Farmer also used the name 'Pop-overs' and wrote that they should be baked in 'hissing hot buttered' pans.[2] The name 'pop-over' is said to have been inspired by the way they popped up over the rim of the cup-cake-size pans in which they were baked. Today, they are less likely to be served at breakfast than as an appetizer at restaurants specializing in steaks and hamburgers.

Batter and Fruit

Probably the best-known batter pudding other than Yorkshire is the French clafoutis. Called a flan or a cake rather than a pudding by the French, it originated in the Limousin region where it consisted of black cherries covered in a sweet pancake (or crêpe) batter and baked. Today other types of cherries, or even other fruits, are used. Similar fruit-enhanced batter puddings also became popular in Britain and in the United States: by the nineteenth century blackberries, cranberries, cherries, plums, apples, stewed prunes and currants were all added to batter to make flavourful puddings.

Most cooks noted that when adding fruit, the batter should be thicker than usual to prevent the fruit from settling at the bottom of the pudding. But Eliza Acton wanted the currants on the bottom – which would be the top when it was turned out – of one of her puddings. It was called 'Black-cap Pudding', and she specified that it should be made with a 'good, light thin batter'. There were many variations on the fruit theme. Some spread a layer of jam or marmalade over the bottom of the pan, poured the batter over it and baked it. When turned out, the pudding would be topped with its own

Black cherry clafoutis is a classic of French home-style cooking.

sauce. Another version, 'Nottingham Pudding', was made by paring and coring apples, filling the cores with sugar and pouring batter over the apples. This was baked until the apples were tender and the batter was crisp and browned.

Pudding Cakes

In Britain and the USA, many eighteenth- and nineteenth-century batter puddings were simply plain batter either boiled in a pudding cloth or baked. Some, called 'Sutherland' or 'castle' puddings, were baked in small pans and when turned out, looked like cupcakes. Eliza Acton added butter and lemon or mace to hers and said: 'When cold they resemble good pound cakes, and may be served as such. Wine sauce should be sent to table with them.'

Elizabeth Raffald made similar 'Little Citron Puddings', baked them in teacups and topped them with sliced citron. Such small batter puddings often had names like 'Pudding Soon Made' or 'Minute Pudding'. Plain batter puddings were usually served with stewed fruit or with a sweet sauce, prompting May Byron, author of *Puddings, Pastries and Sweet Dishes*, to write the following:

> A very plain and not too interesting pudding may be redeemed and transmogrified by the addition of a good sauce; a very rich one may be modified, and a medium one may be greatly enhanced.[3]

Typical sauces were mixtures of butter, sugar and wine; butter and sugar; and, in the US, molasses and butter. Mrs Beeton topped one of her batter puddings with orange marmalade. Recipes recommended that the puddings be served as soon as they were turned out of the pan because they would sink and become heavy if they were left to stand. In fact, Dorothy Hartley wrote of her modern version of a batter pudding, 'Turn it out onto a hot dish and serve it *instantly* (it becomes like leather cold)' in her survey of traditional English cookery, *Food in England* (1954).[4]

Similar cake-like puddings, called 'cottage puddings' were common in nineteenth- and early twentieth-century American cookbooks. Sometimes they were perfectly plain cakes, served with a warm lemon or other sweet sauce, as Byron noted. Often, as with the earlier English puddings, fruits were mixed with the batter before baking. Alternatively, the batter was poured over a layer of sliced, sweetened apples and baked. Many recipes called for the addition of baking soda and cream of tartar or baking powder. These were recognized more as cake than pudding in the twentieth century when Fannie Farmer wrote: 'Cottage Puddings are made of plain cake, served warm with a sauce. Bake in plain cake pans, angel-cake pans, or muffin pans.' She recommended serving them with a vanilla, lemon, orange, raspberry or hard sauce or with stewed fruit. Topping them with whipped cream was, she wrote, 'optional'.[5]

Saucer Puddings

Dorothy Hartley also wrote about unusual small batter puddings she called 'Tewkesbury Saucer Batters (quick and easy snack meals)'.

> Around Tewkesbury and the fruit-picking districts, they make delicious 'saucer batters' for teatime. The woman pickers bring a handful of any soft fruit back from the

In paradise, the mountains are made of pudding. This anonymous etching of *c.* 1670 depicts the Land of Cockaigne.

fields, collect an egg, and the whole dish is ready by the time the kettle boils.

To make them, the cook made a simple batter, poured it into two hot, buttered, saucer-like pans and baked them for about ten minutes. They heated the fruit and sugar separately. As soon as the batters were cooked, they turned them out of their pans and sandwiched them together with the fruit in the middle. They sprinkled sugar on top of the pudding and served them 'instantly' as a sweet teatime treat.

10

Vegetable Pudding

Pease pudding hot, pease pudding cold,
Pease pudding in the pot, nine days old.
Nursery rhyme, eighteenth century

Thanks to Mother Goose, we know puddings and porridges have long been made with peas. Less well known are the puddings made with such plants as potatoes, squash, carrots, spinach, parsley, marigolds, chestnuts, corn and yams. Many of these puddings have been forgotten, but some survive and are even celebrated.

The legendary pease pudding was pease porridge until the pudding cloth came into use in the seventeenth century. But the pease were not fresh springtime peas; rather, they were dried, split green peas, which could be used all year long. To make the pudding, the peas were soaked in water overnight; the next day they were boiled, drained and sieved. Then they were mixed with butter, eggs and seasonings, tied up in a pudding cloth and boiled for an hour or so. The dish was served hot, with pork or bacon if the family had any; leftovers were sliced up and reheated or just served cold, as the rhyme suggests. Pease pudding was nothing if not economical.

A watercolour of 1774 by Gabriel Bray shows British marines on the deck of the *Pallas* dining on pease pudding.

At the time, puddings were not only made from vegetables; they were made in vegetables. Cooks hollowed out carrots, turnips and cucumbers and filled them with mixtures of grated bread, shredded meat, fruit, sugar and spices and baked them. These puddings were the stuff of elegant, rather than thrifty, dining. Robert May stuffed a muskmelon with a pudding made with grated bread, almonds, rose water, sugar, egg yolks, spices and herbs. He wrote that the same filling could be used with cucumbers, cauliflowers, cabbage, parsnips, turnips, carrots or 'great Onions'.

Springtime Puddings

Long before science recognized the nutritional need for vitamins, ordinary people hungered for fresh spring greens at the end of long winters without them. In fact, up to the nineteenth century, many people developed scurvy during the winter, so greens were more than simply a seasonal treat: they were a health food. Cooks gathered wild greens and added them to puddings made with oatmeal or with breadcrumbs. Generally they boiled the puddings in a cloth, but some were baked.

In the northwest of England, a herb pudding called Easter-ledge or ledge pudding was made in springtime from the bistort plant, also known as 'ledge' or 'dock'. The leaves were believed to have both magical and medicinal properties and were thought to prevent miscarriages and purify the blood. The leaves of the herb 'lady's mantle' were also used

Westminster Abbey choristers celebrate Easter with processions and puddings.

as an ingredient in green puddings. They were considered magical because of the way the leaves held shining drops of dew. Ledge pudding was traditionally made by mixing an assortment of leaves with oatmeal, barley, salt and water and letting it all soak overnight. The next day, the mixture was drained, poured into a pudding dish and baked. In another version the leaves were poached, then mixed with eggs and scrambled. The pudding was served at Easter, with bacon, veal or lamb.[1]

A variation called dock pudding was made with dock leaves, spring onions, nettles and herbs along with oatmeal and butter. Traditionally it was served for breakfast, alongside bacon and eggs. Fearing that the pudding was becoming an endangered species, the townsfolk of Mytholmroyd in Calderdale, West Yorkshire held a dock pudding cooking competition in 1971. It has become an annual spring celebration and the pudding lives on. During the Edwardian period the humble herb pudding was reinvented as the elegant guard of honour pudding. It was placed between racks of lamb criss-crossed like swords at a military wedding and roasted. The pudding itself was still made with oatmeal or bread combined with such greens as parsley, spinach and leeks.

Vegetables on every table

Vegetable puddings were served both upstairs and downstairs. Upstairs, there was time and money enough for fanciful preparations like Guard of Honour or Hannah Wolley's green pudding. Wolley, author of *The Queen-like Closet* (2nd edition 1672), made a green pudding with cream, eggs, grated bread and spinach. After it was cooked and turned out of the cloth, she stuck it with split blanched almonds, then poured

Everywhere the English go, puddings are sure to follow, as depicted in this pen and ink illustration by Randolph Caldecott.

a sauce made with butter, wine and sugar over it. She said it would look like a hedgehog.[2]

Richard Bradley's eighteenth-century cookbook, *The Country Housewife and Lady's Director*, included a recipe for a boiled cabbage pudding made with equal parts of finely chopped beef and cabbage, along with eggs, breadcrumbs and seasoning. The recipe was contributed by 'a Gentlewoman in Suffolk' who wrote, 'It may as well be made by People of the lower as of the higher Rank'.[3] Maria Rundell, a mid-nineteenth-century English cookbook author, made a relatively thrifty green bean pudding that combined boiled 'old beans' with pepper, salt, cream and an egg yolk along with spinach juice for added colour. After boiling it in a basin, she poured parsley and butter over it and served it with bacon.[4]

Vegetables such as potatoes, carrots and spinach were also used as a frugal way to thicken puddings, rather than as a main ingredient. Eliza Acton made a vegetable 'plum pudding' that included mashed potatoes and carrots as well as flour, currants, raisins, suet, sugar and spices. She called the pudding 'Cheap and good!' but said it would be less likely to break when turned out of the cloth if eggs were added. Carrots were especially popular pudding vegetables. John Evelyn's *Aceteria: A Discourse of Sallets*, published in London in 1699, included a baked carrot pudding in addition to his many 'sallets', or salads. The carrots were to be grated and combined with eggs, butter, cream, sugar and spices, and thickened with grated bread. He wrote that the recipe was 'a composition for any root pudding'. Similar carrot puddings were common in eighteenth-century England. Usually they were pudding-pies, baked in a pan lined with pastry.

In America, Amelia Simmons included recipes for pumpkin, potato, carrot and winter squash puddings in her cookbook. Following the squash pudding recipe she wrote:

> The above is a good receipt for Pompkins, Potatoes or Yams, adding more moistening or milk and rose water, and to the two latter a few black or Lisbon currants, or dry whortleberries scattered in, will make it better.

Simmons's carrot pudding combined boiled and strained carrots, eggs, sugar, butter, cinnamon and rose water. She wrote that the mixture should be baked in a deep dish, without a crust.[5] Carrot puddings were not unique to the English and Americans. The classic nineteenth-century Russian cookbook, Elena Molokhovets's *A Gift to Young Housewives* (1861), included a recipe for carrot pudding that was very similar to Simmons's, except that it was steamed rather than baked and did not call for rose water.

Savoury and Sweet

Many vegetable puddings contained a small amount of sugar, but were nevertheless intended to be served as savoury puddings. When larger amounts of sugar and/or molasses, raisins, candied citron, cinnamon, cloves, nutmeg and allspice were added to the basic mixtures, the puddings were transformed into desserts. In North America today, sweetened squash, pumpkin and sweet potato mixtures are frequently served as savoury autumn pies rather than puddings, while carrots are more apt to be mixed into cakes and muffins.

American puddings made with cornmeal – hasty or Indian puddings – are well known. But puddings made with fresh corn were also popular, both in North and South America. In fact, they are among the few vegetable puddings made today. A savoury New England corn pudding combines fresh corn kernels with eggs, cream, flour, salt and pepper. It's baked and served as a side dish. In South America, sweet corn puddings are favoured. A Brazilian corn pudding, *curau de milho verde*, is made with puréed corn, milk, sugar and cinnamon, stirred like a hasty pudding. In Peru, a stirred corn pudding is made with dried purple corn, along with pineapple, dried fruits, apple, cinnamon, cloves, sugar, lime juice and corn starch. Called *mazamorra morada*, it's served sprinkled with cinnamon.

A Vietnamese dessert pudding, *che bap*, is made with corn, rice or tapioca, sugar and such options as sesame seeds or pandan leaf. It is served with coconut cream sauce. Though not generally thought of as such, Italy's *sformato* (literally 'unmoulded') is a savoury pudding. *Sformati* are made with cooked and puréed vegetables such as spinach or aubergine (eggplant) combined with breadcrumbs or a béchamel sauce, eggs, cheese, sometimes meat or fish, and seasonings. The mixture is baked in a mould, usually in a bain-marie, and turned out for serving, just like an English pudding.

II

The Once and Future Pudding

The proof of the pudding is in the eating.

Attributed to William Camden, *Remaines of a Greater Worke Concerning Britaine*, 1605

Once upon a time, puddings were nearly ubiquitous in Britain. Many families ate at least one a day. Schools, inns, pubs and restaurants all served their own special puddings. Both published and manuscript cookbooks included dozens of recipes, from holiday extravaganzas to 'last-minute pudding'. Families wrapped up puddings and sent them off to sons and daughters in every corner of the empire as a reminder of home. There seemed to be an infinite variety of puddings and ways to serve them.

However, after the First World War, new manufacturing technologies made powdered pudding mixes possible and self-service grocers' shops helped popularize them, especially in the United States. The first packaged pudding mixes were the My-T-Fine brand, introduced in 1918. These early 'ready-made' puddings were made by stirring the powder into milk, cooking the mixture until it thickened, and then chilling it. At the time, the Jell-O company, famed for its flavoured gelatin products, disparaged powdered puddings in its advertising.

But by the 1930s, the company had also jumped on the pudding bandwagon. Knox and Royal were among the other pudding brands of the day and popular flavours included chocolate, lemon and banana cream. All of the companies published recipe booklets describing a variety of desserts that could be made easily with packaged puddings, from pies to cake fillings to a French chocolate soufflé.

In the late 1940s, truly instant pudding mixes were introduced. These didn't require any cooking at all: one simply mixed the powder into cold milk. The *New York Times* columnist Jane Nickerson called the Amazo brand 'neatly named', adding that it 'amazed even our own tasters, whose palates . . . are not too easily impressed'. By the mid-twentieth century, puddings had lost their pride of place. For this there were many reasons. For some, improved financial circumstances made filling up with a first-course pudding unnecessary. On the other hand, particularly in Britain, food rationing during the Second World War and beyond made it difficult for home cooks to produce the puddings they loved. In addition, puddings took time to make. Women, especially those who worked outside the home, had become too busy to spend hours waiting for a pudding to steam when they could buy an instant or even tinned pudding and a package of powdered custard sauce that would be ready to eat in a flash. As a result, certain cooking skills were lost, or indeed never developed. How many of us know how to use a pudding cloth today? In his memoir *Toast: The Story of a Boy's Hunger*, cookery author Nigel Slater, who grew up in England during the 1960s, writes fondly of eating tinned Heinz Sponge Pudding at Sunday lunch when he was young. His mother served it topped with Nestlé cream, also from a tin, because she couldn't make custard sauce.

In the USA, recipe book writers recommended such puddings with enthusiasm. The 1963 edition of *The Good*

Housekeeping Cook Book referred to them as 'Pantry-Shelf Steamed Puddings' and said: 'Delicious plum, date, and fig puddings come canned, in small and large sizes.' Making one from scratch seemed hopelessly old-fashioned.

A few traditional puddings stubbornly endured, even in the US. The 1974 edition of *The Family Circle Cookbook* included a group of them in a section tellingly titled 'Collector's Items'. Recipes for old-fashioned Indian and plum puddings continued to appear in community cookbooks; however they were greatly outnumbered by short cut or instant puddings made with pre-made mixes.

Then, just when it looked as though homemade puddings were going the way of the buggy whip, they began making a comeback. As the appetite for local, artisanal and 'slow' food increased, cooks began to reconsider classic puddings. Dissatisfied with the quality of shop-bought and instant pudding,

Spotted dick is a favourite with schoolchildren especially when served, as here, with custard.

enterprising home cooks and chefs started reclaiming the pudding – to improve its quality, restore its reputation and return it to the iconic status it formerly enjoyed. In 1985, a group of British pudding lovers got together and founded a Pudding Club 'to ensure the survival of the species'. Since then, the club has prospered and expanded. It has been featured on the BBC and numerous other television and radio programmes as well as in print. The club has published cookery books and even has its own line of packaged puddings. Its pudding nights attract not only members but visitors from around the world.

In another sign of renewed pudding life, a March 2000 issue of *Gourmet* magazine declared:

> British chefs have rediscovered the 'pud,' that odd collection of boiled, steamed, and baked desserts with funny names – jam roly-poly, tipsy cake, spotted dick – and roots that, some say, go back to biblical times.

The magazine not only printed recipes for spotted dick and jam roly-poly but, more importantly, explained how to render suet and how to make suet pastry dough. It gave its imprimatur to the traditional pudding.

Today cookbooks, food magazines and the blogosphere abound with pudding recipes, both traditional and innovative. Fine dining restaurants on both sides of the Atlantic are featuring savoury as well as sweet puddings. Although few households produce their own blood puddings or haggis today, those prepared in restaurants or sold commercially are often very good. The Sticky Toffee Pudding Company of Austin, Texas, owned by an English baker, is winning awards with a line of puddings that are sold in supermarkets and online. They include sticky toffee, English lemon and sticky

Traditionally boiled in a bag, today jam roly poly is more likely to be baked and served with custard.

ginger. In Britain, Duchy Originals, the company founded in 1990 by the Prince of Wales to promote organic food and sustainable farming, sells its own puddings. At Christmastime, the company produces a plum pudding based on a recipe from the 1930s.

Puddings are in the midst of a minor renaissance. They are more prevalent and better made than they have been in

One of the Pudding Club's favourites – sticky toffee pudding.

years. However, it would be an exaggeration to say that their resurgence means pudding has regained its former ubiquitous place on the table. It has not. We should be grateful that it hasn't. It means we no longer need to fill up on stodgy suet pudding because we can't afford meat. Children don't have to suffer through plain rice pudding (again!) for dinner; they can enjoy real, varied meals alongside the grown-ups. Parsimonious reformers no longer recommend cutting costs by feeding cheaply made hasty pudding to poor people. Writers don't need to apologize for pudding nor defend it by resorting to jingoism or grandiosity.

Now we can simply enjoy puddings for what they are. We can revel in the taste of a lovely queen of pudding at the conclusion of a special dinner, treat ourselves to a breakfast complete with a rich blood pudding, or bring warmth to winter and delight to children with a blazing plum pudding. We can celebrate pudding time – again.

Recipes

O lady fair, so sweet and true,
I have a secret charm for you,
To keep your lover's heart your own
When youth is gone, and beauty flown

Though fortune frown and skies are drear,
And friends are changing year by year,
One thing is always sure to please,
Just give him puddings such as these.

Susan Anna Brown, *The Book of Forty Puddings*, 1882

Historical recipes

To make Blood Puddings

—from Gervase Markham, *The English Hus-Wife* (1675).
A nearly identical recipe appeared in Robert May's
The Accomplisht Cook in 1685.

Take the blood of a hogg while it is warm, and steep in it a quart
or more of great Oat-meal grotes, and at the end of three daies
with your hands take the grotes out of the blood, and drain them
clean; then put to those grotes more than a quart of the best Cream
warm'd on the fire; then take some mother of Thyme, Parsley,

Spinage, Succory [chicory], Endive, Sorrel and Strawberry leaves, of each a few chopt exceeding small, and mix them with the grotes, and also a little Fennel-seed finely beaten, then adde a little Pepper, Cloves and Mace, Salt, and great store of suet finely shred, and well beaten; then therewith fill your Forms, and boyl them, as hath been before described.

Dripping Pudding
—from *The Whole Duty of a Woman*, anonymously published in 1737. This is generally considered the first recipe for what we now call Yorkshire pudding.

Make a good batter as for pancakes; put in a hot toss-pan over the fire with a bit of butter to fry the bottom a little then put the pan and butter under a shoulder of mutton, instead of a dripping pan, keeping frequently shaking it by the handle and it will be light and savoury, and fit to take up when your mutton is enough; then turn it in a dish and serve it hot.

After-Thought Pudding
—from Susan Anna Brown, *The Book of Forty Puddings* (1882)

One pint of nice apple sauce sweetened to taste. The yolks of two eggs beaten with it. Put into a buttered dish and bake ten or fifteen minutes. Beat the whites of the eggs stiff, and add half a cup of fine sugar. Spread this meringue on the top and return to the oven to brown.

Christmas Pudding
—from *Godey's Lady's Book and Magazine* (1857)

To bread crumbs and flour, three ounces of each;
Add three eggs and six ounces of suet
Chopped fine, and one-sixth of a nutmeg or more,

So long as you don't over do it.
A good pinch of mace, and of cinnamon ground,
Or in other words carefully grated;
Half a pint of new milk, a spoonful of salt –
A teaspoon I ought to have stated.
To this add some raisins (Malaga) well stoned,
And some currants washed clean and washed nicely,
Of each half a pound, or as some people say,
Of either eight ounces precisely,
Then of citron and lemon an ounce and a half,
Half the former, and one of the latter;
Four ounces of sugar – the moist kind will do –
Which will form an exceeding rich batter
Or mixture. The eggs to a cream should be beat
With the spices, and then by degrees
The milk may be added according to taste,
And the other ingredients to please.
Now taking for granted the pudding is made,
And the water is boiling like fun;
Tie it up in a cloth, pop it into the pot,
And boil – seven hours – till done.

Gilding the Lily

No matter how rich the pudding, cooks often recommended serving them with sauces, custards or creams such as these. Today, a scoop of ice cream is a typical topping.

Plum-Pudding Sauce
—from Mrs Isabella Beeton, *The Book of Household Management* (1861).

Ingredients: 1 wineglassful of brandy, 2 oz of very fresh butter, 1 glass of Madeira, pounded sugar to taste.

Mode: Put the pounded sugar in a basin, with part of the brandy and the butter; let it stand by the side of the fire until it is warm and the sugar and butter are dissolved; then add the rest of the brandy, with the Madeira. Either pour it over the pudding, or serve in a tureen. This is a very rich and excellent sauce.

A German Custard Pudding-Sauce

—from Eliza Acton, *Modern Cookery for Private Families* (1864)

Boil very gently together half a pint of new milk or of milk and cream mixed, a very thin strip or two of fresh lemon-rind, a bit of cinnamon, half an inch of a vanilla bean, and an ounce and a half or two ounces of sugar, until the milk is strongly flavoured; then strain, and pour it, by slow degrees, to the well-beaten yolks of three eggs, smoothly mixed with a knife-end-full (about half a teaspoonful) of flour, a grain or two of salt, and a tablespoonful of cold milk; and stir these very quickly round as the milk is added. Put the sauce again into the stewpan, and whisk or stir it rapidly until it thickens, and looks creamy. It must not be placed upon the fire, but should be held over it, when this is done.

The Germans mill their sauces to a froth; but they may be whisked with almost equally good effect, though a small mill for the purpose – formed like a chocolate mill – may be had at a very trifling cost.

Hard Sauce

—from Jane Cunningham Croly, *Jenny June's American Cookery Book* (1870)

This is made simply by stirring together to a light cream two cups of pounded loaf sugar to half of a large cup of sweet butter. It may be flavored according to taste. For cream and plain batter pudding it may be thinned with a few spoonsful of boiling water and flavored with vanilla. Nutmeg is the best flavor for apple puddings. For rice puddings a little lemon juice or wine may be added.

Wine Sauce
—from Jane Cunningham Croly, *Jenny June's American Cookery Book*
(1870)

Take half a cup of butter and two cups of sugar, beat them together and mix in slowly a cup of wine; melt all over steam but do not stir it while melting.

Snow-Drift Sauce
—from Susan Anna Brown, *The Book of Forty Puddings* (1882)

Half a cup of butter, beaten until white, one cup of pulverized sugar, stirred in gradually and beaten to a cream. Pile it on a glass dish, grate a little nutmeg over it, and set it where it will cool.

Lemon Sauce
—from Rufus Estes, *Good Things to Eat* (1911)

Grate the rind and squeeze the juice of one lemon. Mix together three teaspoons corn starch, one cup of sugar and two cups of boiling water, and cook ten minutes, stirring constantly. Add the lemon rind and juice and one teaspoon of butter.

Modern Recipes

Indian-Meal Pudding (slow cooker version)
—from Kathleen Wall, Colonial Foodways Culinarian, at Plimoth Plantation, Plymouth, Massachusetts. The pudding is always served on 13 November, National Indian Pudding Day.

3 cups (700 ml) milk
½ cup (90 g) cornmeal
½ teaspoon salt

2 tablespoons butter or more
2 eggs
1⅓ cup (110 g) molasses
1 teaspoon cinnamon
½ teaspoon ground ginger
optional: ½ cup (90 g) dried cranberries

Butter the inside of the cooker and preheat on high for 15 minutes. Whisk milk, cornmeal and salt in large heavy-bottomed pot and bring to a boil. (It will rise up somewhat as it heats, so give yourself lots of room unless you like cleaning scorched milk off your stovetop.) After it comes to a boil, continue whisking for another 5 minutes. Cover and simmer on a low heat for 10 minutes and then take off the heat. Add the butter.

Combine eggs, molasses and spices. Take some of the hot cornmeal mixture and add it to the egg mixture to temper it. Then combine both into the pot. Stir in cranberries, if using. (At this point you can top this with plastic wrap, cool and refrigerate for up to 24 hours and then continue.) Scrape into the buttered slow cooker and cook on high for 2–3 hours or on low for 6–8. It will be firmer around the edges than the centre.

Serve warm with ice cream, whipped cream or light cream. Leftovers make a great breakfast.

Lemon Sponge Pudding

Versions of this pudding abound, and no wonder. It's tasty, easy to make and while it bakes, it cleverly separates itself into a top layer that's light and spongy and a bottom layer of lemon custard.

⅔ cup (120 g) granulated sugar
¼ cup (35 g) flour
pinch of salt
3 large eggs, separated
1 cup (240 ml) milk
¼ cup (60 ml) fresh lemon juice

1 tablespoon grated lemon zest
butter

Preheat oven to 170°C/325°F. Butter a 1–1½-quart (1–1½-l) baking dish. In a bowl, mix the sugar, flour and salt together. In a separate bowl, whisk egg yolks, milk, lemon juice and zest together. Combine the two mixtures and stir until well blended.

Beat the egg whites until they hold soft peaks. Blend a small amount of egg whites into the lemon mixture, then gently fold in the rest. Pour the mixture into the buttered baking dish. Place the dish in a larger pan and pour hot water into the larger pan. The water should come about halfway up the sides of the baking dish. Bake for about 35 minutes until the top of the pudding is golden brown. The bottom will be the consistency of a soft custard. Let it cool for around 15 minutes; serve warm or at room temperature.
Serves 4–5.

Eve's Pudding

This is my take on a pudding that's popular on both sides of the pond. It's a simple apple pudding (of course) with a sponge topping.

3 cooking apples
grated zest of 1 lemon
2 tablespoons lemon juice
½ cup (85 g) brown sugar
1 teaspoon cinnamon
½ cup (110 g) butter
½ cup (100 g) granulated sugar
1 large egg
1 cup (140 g) flour
1 teaspoon baking powder
¼ teaspoon salt
¼ cup (60 ml) milk

Preheat the oven to 180°C/350°F. Lightly butter a 1½–2-quart (1½–2-l) baking dish. Set aside. Peel, core and slice the apples thinly. Put them in a bowl and add the lemon zest, lemon juice, brown sugar and cinnamon. Stir together and then tip the mixture into the buttered baking dish.

Cream the butter together with the granulated sugar until light and fluffy. Beat in the egg, mixing it in well. Whisk together the flour, baking powder and salt and mix into the egg mixture alternately with the milk. Spread the batter over top of the apples in the baking dish. Bake for 40 to 45 minutes until the top is golden brown. Serve warm with cream, crème fraiche or ice cream. Serves 6.

Sholeh Zard (Persian Rice Pudding)
—from Simin Bayat-Makou of Makou, Iran.
This is the Makou family's favourite rice pudding.

6 cups (1.4 l) water
1 cup (200 g) Thai jasmine rice*
2 tablespoons vegetable oil
¾ cup (150 g) sugar, or to taste
1 teaspoon saffron, crushed and dissolved in 2 tablespoons hot water
3 tablespoons rose water
¼ cup (25 g) slivered almonds
1 teaspoon cinnamon
4 tablespoons chopped pistachios

Rinse the rice thoroughly, then pour into a large, heavy saucepan and add 6 cups of warm water. Soak overnight. Then, using the same water, bring to a boil. Reduce to a slow simmer and cook the rice, stirring gently until it softens, about 30 minutes. If necessary, add more water. Stir in the oil and sugar. Taste and add additional sugar if it is not sweet enough. Continue to cook, stirring constantly, until the sugar is melted and the rice is completely soft, another 20 minutes or so. Stir in the saffron, slivered almonds and rose water. Be sure to continue stirring long enough to incorporate the saffron completely. The mixture should have thickened and the rice should be a rich, appetizing shade of pale gold.

Pour into three small serving bowls and let cool. (If it is poured into one large serving bowl, the pudding has a tendency to become watery.) When the pudding has cooled sufficiently, decorate the top with cinnamon and pistachios. In Iran, it is customary to make a pattern of criss-crossed lines with the cinnamon and nuts rather than sprinkling them over the entire surface. Serve at room temperature, or refrigerate and serve chilled.

*Although many recipes for sholeh zard call for basmati rice, the Makou family feels strongly that it is too soft for the pudding. They insist on Thai jasmine rice.

Corn Pudding

A contemporary version of an American vegetable pudding and an excellent side dish on a Thanksgiving table.

4 tablespoons butter, melted and cooled
2 eggs
¼ cup (35 g) flour
1 teaspoon salt
½ teaspoon pepper
1 cup (240 ml) milk
2 cups (150 g) sweetcorn
¼ cup (25 g) grated Parmesan, Pecorino or other hard cheese

Preheat oven to 180°C/350°F. Grease a 1½-quart (1½-l) baking dish. Melt butter and set aside to cool. Whisk eggs together, then add the flour, salt and pepper and mix well. Stir in the milk and melted butter. Add the sweetcorn. Pour into the greased baking dish and sprinkle the grated cheese over the top. Place the baking dish in a larger pan. Pour hot water into the larger pan until it comes about halfway up the sides of the baking dish.

Bake for about 1 hour, or until the top is golden brown and a toothpick inserted in the centre of the pudding comes out clean. Serves 4–6.

Pouding chômeur (Poor Man's Pudding)

—from Christiane Reid of Montreal. This economical pudding was a Depression-era dessert in Quebec. Over time, it has become a family favourite.

Dough
1½ cups (140–210 g) flour
1 teaspoon baking powder
¼ cup (55 g) butter
1 cup (200 g) granulated sugar
1 cup (240 ml) milk

Sauce
2 cups (480 ml) water
2 cups (340 g) brown sugar
¼ cup (55 g) butter

Preheat the oven to 170°C/325°F. Butter a 13 x 9-inch (35 x 25 cm) baking pan. Sift the flour and baking powder together and set aside. In a bowl, beat the butter until creamy, then gradually add the sugar until the mixture is smooth. Gradually incorporate the milk and the flour mixture alternately, mixing thoroughly until all the ingredients are combined. Pour the dough into the buttered pan.

For the sauce, pour the water into a saucepan and bring it to a boil. Stir in the brown sugar and butter. Let the mixture boil briefly, then remove from the heat. Pour the syrup over the dough in the pan – do not mix it into the dough. Bake for about 45 minutes; the top should be golden.

Pudding Humour

Bullet Pudding

I don't know whether Jane Austen ever played this game, but it was popular in her day. Her niece, Fanny Austen Knight, described the pudding in a letter to her friend Dorothy Chapman in 1804.

I was surprised that you did not know what a Bullet Pudding is but as you don't I will endeavour to describe it as follows: You must have a large pewter dish filled with flour which you must pile up into a sort of pudding with a peak at the top, you must then lay a Bullet at the top & everybody cuts a slice of it & the person that is cutting it when the Bullet falls must poke about with their nose & chins till they find it & then take it out with their mouths which makes them strange figures all covered with flour but the worst is that you must not laugh for fear of the flour getting up your nose & mouth & choking you. You must not use your hands in taking the bullet out.

References

A man may receive more solid Satisfaction from Pudding,
while he is living, than from Praise, after he is dead.
Benjamin Franklin, *Poor Richard's Almanack*, 1750

Introduction

1 M.F.K. Fisher, *With Bold Knife and Fork* (New York, 1996),
  p. 255.
2 Quoted in C. Anne Wilson, *Food and Drink in Britain: From
  the Stone Age to the 19th Century* (Chicago, IL, 1991), p. 321.

1 A Pudding Chronology

1 Attributed to Henry Carey, *A Learned Dissertation on
  Dumpling* (Los Angeles, CA, 1970), p. 4.
2 Kenelm Digby, *The Closet of Sir Kenelm Digby Knight Opened*
  (Project Guttenberg ebook, 2005), p. 180.

2 Pudding in Black and White

1 Robert May, *The Accomplisht Cook* (London, 1685), p. 26.

3 Meat Pudding

1 Hannah Glasse, *The Art of Cookery Made Plain and Easy* (Hamden, CT, 1971), p. 85.
2 Richard Bradley, *The Country Housewife and Lady's Director* (London, 1980), pp. 122–3.

4 Suet Pudding

1 Stephen Mennell, *All Manners of Food* (New York, 1985), p. 242.
2 Laura Mason and Catherine Brown, *Traditional Foods of Britain* (Totnes, Devon, 1999), p. 252.
3 Jane Cunningham Croly, *Jenny June's American Cookery Book* (New York, 1870), p. 329.

5 Christmas Pudding

1 Sarah Josepha Hale, *The Good Housekeeper: or, The Way to Live Well and Be Well* (Boston, 1839), pp. 67–8.
2 Estelle Woods Wilcox, *Buckeye Cookery and Practical Housekeeping* (Minneapolis, MN, 1877), p. 204.

6 Hasty Pudding

1 Thomas Heywood, *The English Traveller*, vol. IV (London, 1874), available at http://books.google.com/books, accessed 1 March 2012.
2 David McCullough, *John Adams* (New York, 2001), pp. 597–8.
3 Count Rumford, 'An Essay on Food', in Judith Herman and Marguerite Shalett Herman, *The Cornucopia* (New York, 1973), pp. 256–8.
4 Isabella Beeton, *The Book of Household Management* (New York, 1968), p. 606.

7 Bread Pudding

1 *The Goodman of Paris (Le Ménagier de Paris)*, trans. Eileen Power (New York, 1928), p. 276.
2 Mrs A.D.T. Whitney, *Just How: A Key to the Cook-Books* (Boston, 1880), p. 214.
3 Colin Spencer, *British Food: An Extraordinary Thousand Years of History* (New York, 2002), p. 128.
4 Alberto Alvaro Ríos, *Capirotada: A Nogales Memoir* (Albuquerque, NM, 1999), pp. 85–7.

8 Rice Pudding

1 Gervase Markham, *The English-Hus-Wife* (London, 1675), bk 2, p. 60.
2 Urbain Dubois, *Artistic Cookery: A Practical System for the use of the Nobility and Gentry and for Public Entertainments* (London, 1887), p. 20.

9 Batter Pudding

1 Mary Newton Foote Henderson, *Practical Cooking and Dinner Giving* (New York, 1877), p. 71.
2 Fannie Farmer, *The Boston Cooking-School Cookbook* (Boston, MA, 1896), p. 76.
3 May Byron, *Puddings, Pastries and Sweet Dishes* (London, 1929), p. 308.
4 Dorothy Hartley, *Food in England* (London, 1954), pp. 617–18.
5 Farmer, *Boston Cooking-School*, p. 570.

10 Vegetable Pudding

1 Laura Mason and Catherine Brown, *Traditional Foods of Britain* (Totnes, Devon, 1999), pp. 55–6.

2 Hannah Wolley, *The Queen-like Closet* (London, 1672), p. 249.

3 Richard Bradley, *The Country Housewife and Lady's Director* (London, 1980), p. 14.

4 Maria Eliza Rundell, *A New System of Domestic Cookery* (Boston, MA, 1807), p. 143.

5 Amelia Simmons, *The First American Cookbook: A Facsimile of 'American Cookery', 1796* (New York, 1958), pp. 27–8.

Select Bibliography

What is Poetry, but a Pudding of Words.
Attributed to Henry Carey,
A Learned Dissertation on Dumpling, 1726

Acton, Eliza, *Modern Cookery for Private Families* (London, 1864)

Beeton, Isabella, *The Book of Household Management*, facsimile reprint of 1861 edition (New York, 1968)

Bradley, Richard, *The Country Housewife and Lady's Director*, facsimile reprint of 1736 edition (London, 1980)

Brears, Peter, *All The King's Cooks* (London, 1999)

Brown, Susan Anna, *The Book of Forty Puddings* (New York, 1882)

Byron, May, *Puddings, Pastries and Sweet Dishes* (London, 1929)

Carey, Henry (attrib.), *A Learned Dissertation on Dumpling*, facsimile reprint of 1727 edition (Los Angeles, CA, 1970)

Coe, Sophie, manuscript cookbook collection, 1704–1924, at Schlesinger Library, Cambridge, MA

Davidson, Alan, *The Oxford Companion to Food* (Oxford, 1999)

Fitzgibbon, Theodora, *A Taste of London* (Boston, 1975)

Glasse, Hannah, *The Art of Cookery Made Plain and Easy*, facsimile reprint of 1796 edition (Hamden, CT, 1971)

Hartley, Dorothy, *Food in England* (London, 1954)

Mason, Laura, and Catherine Brown, *Traditional Foods of Britain* (Totnes, Devon, 1999)

Murrey, Thomas J., *Puddings and Dainty Desserts* (New York, 1886)

Paston-Williams, Sara, *The National Trust Book of Traditional Puddings* (London, 1986)

Pool, Daniel, *What Jane Austen Ate and Charles Dickens Knew* (New York, 1993)

Saberi, Helen, *A Pudding Book* (Ludlow, Shropshire, 2006)

De Salis, Mrs (Harriet Anne), *Puddings and Pastry à la Mode* (London, 1893)

Sherman, Sandra, 'English Nationalism', *Petits propos culinaires*, 78 (Totnes, Devon, 2005)

Simmons, Amelia, *The First American Cookbook: A Facsimile of 'American Cookery', 1796* (New York, 1958)

Smith, Andrew, *The Oxford Encyclopedia of Food and Drink in America* (Oxford, 2004)

Thomas, Helen, *The Pudding Book* (London, 1980)

Thompson, Flora, *Lark Rise to Candleford* (Boston, MA, 2009)

Turner, Keith, and Jean Turner, *The Pudding Club Book* (London, 1997)

Wilson, C. Anne, *Food and Drink in Britain: From the Stone Age to the 19th Century* (Chicago, IL, 1991)

Websites and Associations

Feeding America
http://digital.lib.msu.edu/projects/cookbooks

Fons Grewe Digital Collection, University of Barcelona
www.bib.ub.edu/fileadmin/imatges/llibres/grewe.htm

Food Timeline
www.foodtimeline.org

Historic Food
www.historicfood.com

The Pudding Club
www.puddingclub.com

Pudding Hollow Pudding Festival
www.puddingcontest.wordpress.com

What's Cooking America
www.whatscookingamerica.net

Acknowledgements

Writing a book is an excellent way to remind yourself of just how generous and thoughtful people can be. Friends, relatives and acquaintances all gladly shared their pudding books, reminiscences, recipes and suggestions with me. And so did people I've only met through the Internet, which is even more impressive and inspiring.

I would like to particularly thank Andy Smith, Joe Carlin, Patricia Kelly, Barbara Ketcham Wheaton, Kathleen Wall, Jacqueline and Parviz Amirhor, Lola MacLeod, Lila Fanger, Anne Faulkner, Nancy Stutzman, Christiane Reid, Simin Bayat-Makou, Sandra Sherman, Mary Lou Nye, Tracy Claros, Debbie Pierce, Winnie Williams and Dan Coleman. I am also indebted to the staff and librarians at the Schlesinger Library at Harvard for their patience as well as their knowledge.

The members of my writing workshop deserve a special thank you for diligently reading every word and improving a great many of them. They are: Myrna Kaye, Roberta Leviton, Barbara Mende, Sabra Morton, Shirley Moskow, Beth Surdut, Molly Turner and Rose Yesu.

Thank you all.

Photo Acknowledgements

The author and the publishers wish to express their thanks to the below sources of illustrative material and/or permission to reproduce it:

Author's collection: pp. 9, 13, 20, 21, 64, 65, 68; Bigstock: pp. 36, 43, 52, 54, 80, 84, 97 (Monkey Business Images), 98 (Fotosmurf01), 105, 119, 121 (Monkey Business Images); The Bridgeman Art Library/ 'Pudding Time', plate 6 from *Illustrations of Time*, published 1827 (etching) by George Cruikshank (1792–1878), Fitzwilliam Museum, University of Cambridge, UK: p. 10; British Library, London: p. 19; © The Trustees of the British Museum: pp. 10, 11, 16, 23, 38, 42, 47, 51, 59, 61, 63, 71, 108, 113; courtesy of The Bury Black Pudding Company: pp. 27, 122; Library of Congress: pp. 40, 58, 60, 66; © National Maritime Museum, Greenwich, London: p. 110; The New York Public Library: p. 18; New York Historical Society: p. 81; courtesy of the Pudding Club: pp. 8, 122; Rex Features: pp. 86 (Monkey Business Images), 90 (Woman's Own), 102–3 (Clive Dixon), 111 (Andrew Dunsmore); Schlesinger Library, Radcliffe Institute, Harvard University: p. 24; Shutterstock: pp. 6 (lisasaadphotography), 95 (highviews).

Index

italic numbers refer to illustrations; **bold** to recipes